Turner Publishing Company
Publishers of America's History
P.O. Box 3101
Paducah, Kentucky 42002-3101

Co-published by
Mark A. Thompson, Associate Publisher

For book publishing write to:
M.T. Publishing Company, Inc.
P.O. Box 6802
Evansville, Indiana 47719-6802

Pre-Press work by M.T. Publishing Company, Inc.
Graphic Designers: Elizabeth A. Dennis, Mike Fetch, and Bryan McGuire
Cover Design: Columbus Division of Fire

Copyright © 2002
Columbus Division of Fire

This book or any part thereof may not be reproduced without the written consent of the Columbus Division of Fire and the Publishers.

The materials were compiled and produced using available information. Turner Publishing Company, M.T. Publishing Company, Inc., and the Columbus Division of Fire regret they cannot assume liability for errors or omissions.

Library of Congress
Control Number 2001086836

ISBN: 1-56311-636-7

Printed in the United States of America

Contents

Acknowledgments — 4
Firefighters Memorial — 5
Died in the Line of Duty — 6
Memorial to FDNY — 9
Letter from the Mayor — 10
Letter from the Safety Director — 11
Columbus City Council — 12
Letter from the Fire Chief — 13
Letters from Union Presidents — 14
Fire Chiefs of CFD — 15
Columbus Division of Fire Rank — 16
Introduction — 17
Columbus Division of Fire Bureaus — 23
    Administration Bureau — 24
    Emergency Services Bureau — 25
    Fire Prevention Bureau — 28
    Support Services Bureau — 32
    Training Bureau — 35
    Supplementary Groups of the CDF — 39
Columbus Division of Fire Awards — 50
Columbus Division of Fire Stations — 51
Columbus Division of Fire Officers — 137
Columbus Division of Fire Firefighters — 153
Columbus Division of Fire Civilians — 197

ACKNOWLEDGMENTS

The History Book Committee and the Columbus Ohio Division of Fire would like to thank the following for their help in the production of this publication.

Chief Ned Pettus	FF Jeff Geitter	Auxiliary
Chief Steven Woltz	FF Chris Guay	Box-15
Asst. Chief Joseph Keefer	FF Kevin Harr	Jim Patrick
Asst. Chief Carl Lawhorn	FF Mark Harris	Thomas Brunk
Battalion Chief Mark Devine	FF Robert Phillips	Sonny J. Lewis
Battalion Chief Tommy Hackett	FF Norman Spafford	John Keyt
Captain Greg Lash	FF Bob Throckmorton	Mayor Mike Coleman
Engine House No. 1	Tina Sloan	Safety Director
Engine House No. 10	Sue Levesque	City Council
Captain Steve Heselden	Barb Becker	M.T. Publishing Co., Inc.
Lieutenant Gerald Walker	The Central Ohio Fire Museum	Mark Thompson
Lieutenant Mike Vedra	Dick Byrd	Liz Dennis
FF Steve Cox	4 Unit	Anyone donating photos or
FF Dan Ducharme	IAFF Local 67	information unmentioned

Dedicated To Our Families
— The History Book Committee —
Mike Fetch, Brian McGuire, Bill Hall, Steve Basil

Firefighters Memorial

On the night of February 19, 1936 a raging fire at the old I.O.O.F. Hall at 198 South High Street claimed the lives of two Columbus fire captains, one lieutenant and two firefighters. Two other firefighters were seriously injured and consequently retired from the department.

From the ashes of that tragic fire arose a dream ... the dream of a memorial honoring all firefighters who have answered their Last Alarm. The dream grew slowly and in 1957 came closer to reality as Fire Chief Walter Strickfaden commissioned FF Joe Pishitelli to be project coordinator for the construction of a Firefighters Memorial. Land was acquired through a City Council ordinance and Lieutenant Ed Nothacker was selected to design the Memorial. On November 30, 1957, ground was broken at Marconi Boulevard and Gay Street, and the Firefighters Memorial became more than just a dream.

Using only private funds, Nothacker and Pishitelli worked tirelessly to coordinate construction of the Memorial, with nearly all labor donated by firefighters. The Memorial was anchored by four twelve-foot fluted limestone columns on a six-and-one-half foot base. A bronze tower bell from a former Columbus firehouse was hung between the columns, and a bronze Maltese Cross was placed at the top of the Memorial on each of its four sides. Those crosses, as well as the Memorial's plaques, were cast from melted firehouse bells.

On April 13, 1958, less than five months after the ground breaking, the Memorial was dedicated by Mayor M. E. Sensenbrenner. A thirty-foot aluminum flag pole on a terrazzo base was added in 1965, and during the summer of 1988 firefighters completed a major renovation project. Under the guiding hand of Captain Jim Ross, the original Memorial was refurbished, four matching stone benches were placed around the perimeter of the monument and the grounds were re-landscaped. The funds, materials and labor were provided by members of the Columbus Division of Fire and the Central Ohio community. A black granite monument was added to the site, engraved with the names of all Columbus firefighters who have died in the line of duty. On October 16, 1988, the Firefighters Memorial was re-dedicated with the solemn lighting of the new Eternal Flame.

Today the Firefighters Memorial still stands as proudly as it did at its dedication over thirty-five years ago. Our firefighters' pride is reflected in the Memorial, as firefighters continue to devote both time and energy to its upkeep. And every year the tower bell is tolled at a memorial service held at this beautiful, historic site.

Died In The Line Of Duty

FF Andrew J. Kerins

Capt. Dan S. Lewis

FF Mark Newman
Was killed August 4, 1870 by falling walls at Columbus Woolen Mills, Located on the west side of the canal near Mound Street.

FF Andrew J. Kerins
Of Truck 2, was killed January 2, 1892, at the Booth Mfg. Co. fire on Lazelle Street north of Gay Street.

Lt. William Mclaughlin
Of Hook & Ladder 1, located at Engine House 3 was killed September 14, 1892, when he was thrown from a telegraph pole on North High Street in front of Union Depot while trying to protect the telegraph lines from derrick guys.

Capt. Louis Lang
Of Engine 3, died March 3, 1893, from consumption contracted from exposure at Metropolitan Opera House and Philadelphia Building fire at Rich and High Streets on January 5, 1892. He was the first firefighter to draw a pension check. He only received one check for $20 because of his death.

FF John Hack
Driver of Hose Company 5 died November 25, 1897, from blood poisoning contracted from an injury he received. Veteran of over 3 years.

Capt. Joseph Hecht
Of Engine 11, died May 7, 1898, from injuries received while fighting a fire at the Main Street School. Veteran of 9 years service.

Capt. Dan S. Lewis
Of Hook and Ladder 2, was killed April 26, 1903, at a General Alarm Fire which engulfed the Union Clothing Co., Botts Bros., Kirbys and the Brunson Building when he was buried under falling walls. Veteran of 21 years.

FF George Miller
Of Truck 5, located at Engine House 8 was killed November 15, 1910, while responding to a fire on Hayes Avenue when he fell from his truck breaking his neck. Veteran of 10 years.

FF John M. Evans
Fire Dept. Lineman was killed July 17, 1911, when he fell 40' from a telephone pole on North High Street in front of Union Depot while he was stringing telegraph wires. Veteran of 3 years.

FF C. E. Palmer
Of Engine 7 was killed August 27, 1912, at Broad and Center Streets in a collision between Engine 7 and a street car. Veteran of 1 1/2 years.

Engineer Charles Brehm
Of Engine 12, died September 4, 1917 from injuries he received September 3, 1917 at State and Levee Streets, while attempting to move a steamer closer to a hydrant. The steamer started down an incline into Levee Street. Engineer Brehm realized the steamer could not be stopped and took the pole and steered the steamer into a brick wall. The pole crashed through the wall crushing him between the wall and the steamer. Veteran of over 25 years.

Capt. Charles F. Garrett Sr.
Of 6 Hose Wagon died from injuries received on July 19, 1922, in a collision with an auto while responding to Box 313 at Long and High. Veteran of 27 years.

FF Harlan A. Ruth
Of Engine 5 died February 24, 1923, from injuries received at the Ebner and Hopkins Fire on April 1, 1920, when a large pulley fell from a burning elevator and struck him in the head. Veteran of 11 years.

Capt. Fred Stehle
Of Engine 2 died November 16, 1923, from injuries received on November 11, 1923, at Walnut and Zettler Alleys when he was thrown from a 30' ladder. Veteran of 32 years.

FF Fred Dalton
Of Hose Wagon 6 died on January 10, 1924, from injuries sustained on January 8, 1924, at High and Lynn while responding to Box No. 313 at High and Long Streets. Veteran of 3 years.

FF James Cheeseman
Of 5 Pump was killed July 25, 1925, when a street car collided with 5 Pump at Parsons and Thurman Avenues. Veteran of 14 years.

Eng. Charles Brehm

Capt. Charles F. Garrett, Sr.

FF Harlan A. Ruth

Capt. Fred Stehle

FF James Cheeseman

FF Carl Schroeder

FF Paul J. Altonbach

Bn. Chief Charles Barklow

Capt. W. J. Roop

Capt. Charles Eckstorm

Lt. Henry Myers

FF Herbert Harrington

Capt. Otto Ignatz

FF Oliver Metzger

Lt. Harry McFadden

Capt. Robert Welsh

Capt. John O'Reilly

FF Louis Martin

FF Robert J. Foran

FF Clarence Cox

Capt. Clarence "Freddy" Martin

FF Carl Schroeder
Of 5 Pump died September 3, 1925, as a result of injuries he received on July 25, 1925, when 5 Pump collided with a street car at Parsons and Thurman. Veteran of 23 years.

FF Paul J. Altonbach
Of Engine 6 was killed October 7, 1929, while trying to rescue a man from a well at City Ice and Fuel. When he was half way down into the well he was overcome by "Black Damp" and fell backwards into the well and drowned. Veteran of 5 years.

Bn. Chief Charles Barklow
Killed on February 5, 1931, when his District Chiefs' car and another auto collided at 3rd Avenue and Perry Street while responding to Box 276. Veteran of 33 years.

Capt. Harry Fetter
Of 17 Pump died February 23, 1932 from heart attack while fighting a house fire at 2759 Eakin Road. He was found lying on his back in six inches of water in the basement. Veteran of 33 years.

FF Herbert Harrington
Of Squad 1 was killed February 19, 1936, when a wall collapsed on him at the Odd Fellows Temple fire at Rich and High Streets. Veteran of 4 years.

Capt. Otto Ignatz
Of 3 Pump was killed February 19, 1936, when a wall collapsed on him at the Odd Fellows Temple fire at Rich and High Streets. Veteran of 11 years.

FF Oliver Metzger
Of Squad 1 was killed February 19, 1936, when a wall collapsed on him at the Odd Fellows Temple fire at Rich and High Streets. Veteran of 13 years.

Lt. Harry McFadden
Of 1 Truck was killed February 19, 1936, when a wall collapsed on him at the Odd Fellows Temple fire at Rich and High Streets. Veteran of 16 years.

Capt. Robert Welsh
Of Squad 1 was killed February 19, 1936, when a wall collapsed on him at the Odd Fellows Temple fire at Rich and High Streets. Veteran of 10 years.

FF Charles A. Beatty
Was electrocuted on August 15, 1936, while fighting a fire on 20th Street, north of Long. Veteran of 18 years.

Capt. W. J. Roop
Of 18 Pump died February 26, 1943, as a result of a heart attack he suffered while fighting a fire on 18th Avenue. Veteran of 23 years.

Capt. Charles Eckstorm
Of Squad 1 was killed September 27, 1944, when the Squad he was riding met in a collision with another auto at Livingston and 3rd Streets. Veteran of 21 years.

Lt. Henry Myers
Of 7 Pump died February 1, 1946 from a skull fracture when he slipped on the ice and struck his head on 7 Pump at a fire on Highland Street. Veteran of 21 years.

Capt. John O'Reilly
Of 6 Pump died February 3, 1947 as a result of a heart attack he suffered while fighting a fire at the East Market House on Mt. Vernon Avenue. Veteran of 16 years.

FF Louis Martin
Of 5 Pump was killed May 26, 1948, at Jaeger and Thurman when 5 Pump was struck by a trolley car. Veteran of 31 years.

FF Robert J. Foran
Of 10 Quad was killed on December 4, 1951, when he fell from the Quad while it was responding to an alarm on W. Broad Street. Veteran of 34 Years.

FF Clarence Cox
Of 7 Truck died November 21, 1962, from a heart attack he suffered after returning from a fire run. Veteran of 19 years.

Capt. Clarence "Freddy" Martin
Squad Supervisor drowned in the Olentangy River (in flood stage) on March 22, 1964. His boat overturned below the 5th Avenue dam while trying to rescue two men from the river.

Capt. Paul Casey

FF Chester Fowler

Lt. Jack Russ

FF Maurice Gates

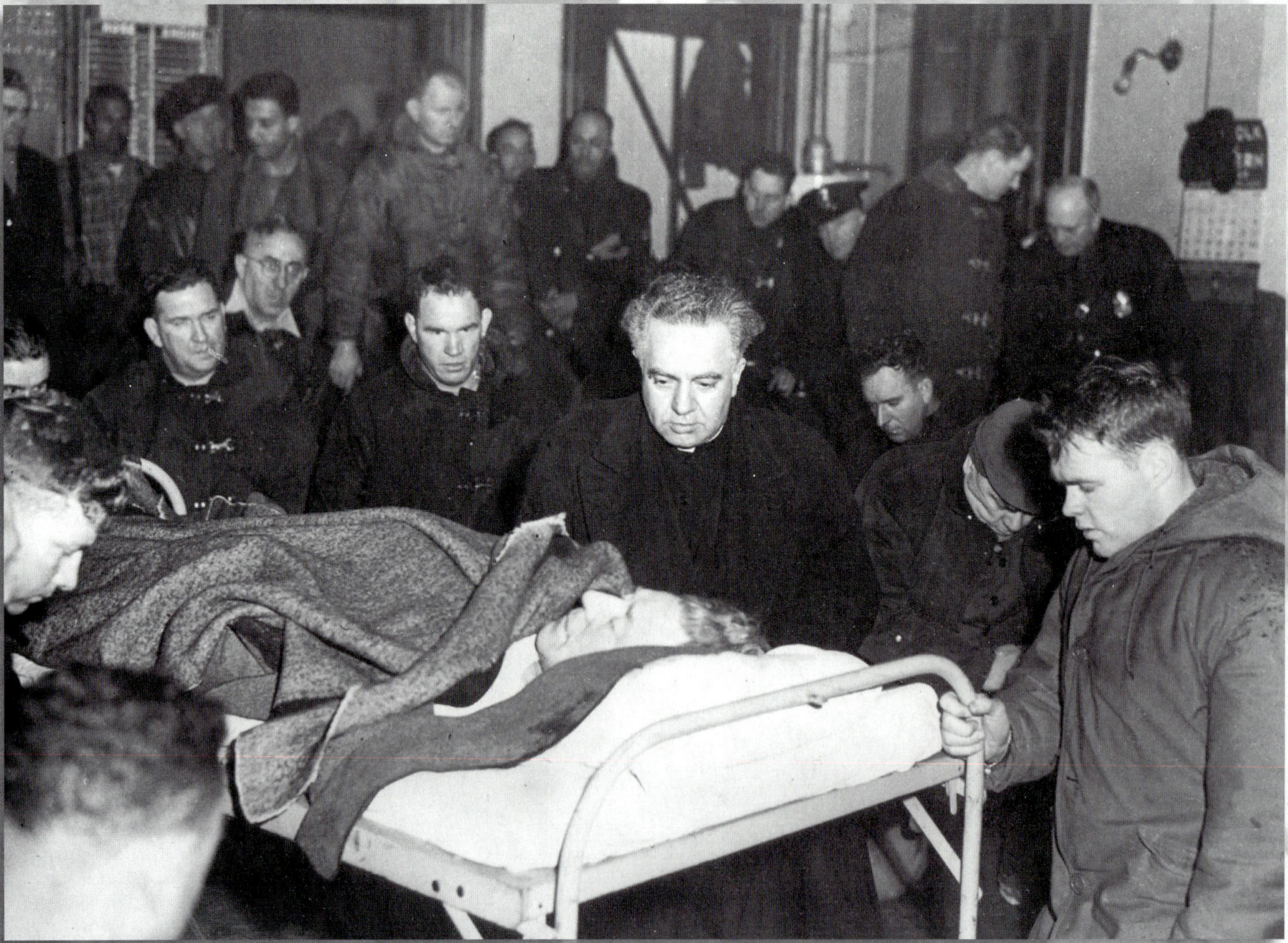

Capt. Paul Casey
Of 10 Truck died October 24, 1964, from a heart attack he suffered while fighting a fire at 1187 W. Broad Street. Veteran of 24 years.

FF Chester Fowler
Of Engine 6 died November 27, 1971, as a result of a heart attack he suffered while fighting a basement fire on Millbank Road. Veteran of 12 years.

Lt. Jerry Kuhn
Of Engine 19 died January 3, 1972, as a result of a heart attack he suffered while fighting a fire at 207 W. Weber Road. Veteran of 13 years.

Lt. Jack Russ
Of Engine 22 died January 24, 1972, as a result of an injury he received on January 15 while fighting a fire at 274 Stockbridge Road. Veteran of 12 years.

FF Maurice Gates
Of Ladder 10 was killed on September 15, 1982, at a warehouse fire at 144 S. Glenwood Avenue. Veteran of 1 year.

FF John W. Nance
Was Acting Lieutenant of Engine 2 and was killed on July 25, 1987, on a 3rd Alarm fire at 151 North High Street after he fell through a hole in the floor into the basement. Veteran of 28 years.

Lt. Jerry Kuhn

FF John W. Nance

Father Schaeffer giving last rites to Capt. John O'Reilly at 8 House. Captain O'Reilly was brought to 8 House from the East Market House fire where he suffered a fatal heart attack.

TO THE FDNY MEMBERS WHO SO BRAVELY MADE THE SUPREME SACRIFICE ON SEPTEMBER 11, 2001

JOSEPH AGNELLO, LT. BRIAN AHERN, ERIC ALLEN, RICHARD ALLEN, CAPT. JAMES AMATO, CALIXTO ANAYA JR., JOSEPH ANGELINI SR. JOSEPH ANGELINI JR., FAUSTINO APOSTOL JR., DAVID ARCE, LOUIS ARENA, CARL ASARO, LT. GREGG ATLAS, GERALD ATWOOD, GERALD BAPTISTE, ASST. CHIEF, GERALD BARBARA, MATTHEW BARNES, ARTHUR BARRY, LT. STEVEN BATES, CARL BEDIGAN, STEPHEN BELSON, JOHN BERGIN, PAUL BEYER, PETER BIELFELD, BRIAN BILCHER, CARL BINI, CHRISTOPHER BLACKWELL, MICHAEL BOCCHINO, FRANK BONOMO, GARY BOX, MICHAEL BOYLE, KEVIN BRAKEN, MICHAEL BRENNAN, CAPT. DANIEL BRETHEL, CAPT. PATRICK BROWN, ANDREW BRUNN, CAPT. VINCENT BRUNTON, RONALD BUCCA, GREG BUCK, CAPT. WILLIAM BURKE JR., ASST. CHIEF DONALD BURNS, JOHN BURNSIDE, THOMAS BUTLER, PATRICK BYRNE, GEORGE CAIN, SALVATORE CALABRO, CAPT. FRANK CALLAHAN, MICHAEL CAMMARATA, BRIAN CANNIZZARO, DENNIS CAREY, MICHAEL CARLO, MICHAEL CARROLL, PETER CARROLL, THOMAS CASORIA, MICHAEL CRAWLEY, VERNON CHERRY, NICHOLAS CHIOFALO, JOHN CHIPURA, MICHAEL CLARKE, STEVEN COAKLEY, TAREL COLEMAN, JOHN COLLINS, ROBERT CORDICE, RUBIN CORREA, JAMES COYLE, ROBERT CRAWFORD, LT. JOHN CRISCI, BATT. CHIEF DENNIS CROSS, THOMAS CULLEN III, ROBERT CURATOLO, LT. EDWARD D'ATRI, MICHAEL D'AURIA, SCOTT DAVIDSON, EDWARD DAY, BATT. CHIEF THOMAS DEANGELIS, MANUAL DELVALLE, MARTIN DEMEO, DAVID DERUBBIO, LT. DESPERITO, BATT. CHIEF DENNIS DEVLIN, GERARD DEWAN, GEORGE DIPASQUALE, LT. KEVIN DONNELLY, LT. KEVIN DOWDELL, BATT. CHIEF RAYMOND DOWNEY, GERARD DUFFY, CAPT. MARTIN EGAN JR., MICHAEL ELFERIS, FRANCIS ESPOSITO, LT. MICHAEL ESPOSITO, ROBERT EVANS, BATT. CHIEF JOHN FANNING II, CAPT. JOHN FARINO, TERRANCE FARRELL, CAPT. JOSEPH FARRELLY, DEPUTY COMM. WILLIAM FEEHAN, LEE FEHLING, ALAN FEINBURG, MICHAEL FIORE, LT. JOHN FISCHER, ANDRE FLETCHER, JOHN FLORIO, LT. MICHAEL FODOR, THOMAS FOLEY, DAVID FONTANA, ROBERT FOTI, ANDREW FREDERICKS, LT.

PETER FREUND, THOMAS GAMBINO JR., CHIEF OF FDNY PETER GANCI JR., LT. CHARLES GARBARINI, THOMAS GARDNER, MATTHEW GARVEY, BRUCE GARY, GARY GEIDEL, BATT. CHIEF EDWARD GERAGHTY, DENIS GERMAIN, LT. VINCENT GIAMMONA, JAMES GIBERSON, RONNIE GEIS, PAUL GILL, LT. JOHN GINLEY, JEFFREY GIORDANO, JOHN GIORDANO, KEITH GLASCOE, JAMES GRAY, BATT. CHIEF JOSEPH GRZELAK, JOSE GUADALUPE, LT. GEOFFREY GUJA, LT. JOSEPH GULLICKSON, DAVID HALDERMAN, LT. VINCENT HALLORAN, ROBERT HAMILTON, SEAN HANLEY, THOMAS HANNEFIN, DANA HANNON, DANIEL HARLIN, LT. HARVEY HARRELL, LT. STEPHEN HARRELL, CAPT. THOMAS HASKELL JR. TIMOTHY HASKELL, CAPT. TERENCE HATTON, MICHAEL HAUB, LT. MICHAEL HEALEY, JOHN HEFFERNAN, RONNIE HENDERSON, JOSEPH HENRY, WILLIAM HENRY, THOMAS HETZEL, CAPT. BRIAN HICKEY, LT. TIMOTHY HIGGINS, JONATHAN HOHMANN, THOMAS HOLOHAN, JOSEPH HUNTER, CAPT. WALTER HYNES, JOSEPH IELPHI, CAPT. FREDERICK III JR., WILLIAM JOHNSTON, ANDREW JORDAN, KARL JOSEPH, LT. ANTHONY JOVIC, ANGEL JUARBE JR., REVEREND MYCHAL JUDGE, VINCENT KANE, BATT. CHIEF CHARLES KASPER, PAUL KEATING, RICHARD KELLY JR., THOMAS R. KELLY, THOMAS KENNEDY, LT. RONALD KERWIN, MICHAEL KIEFER,

ROBERT KING JR. SCOTT KOPYTOK, WILLIAM KRUKOWSKI, KENNETH KUMPEL, THOMAS KUVEIKIS, DAVID LAFORGE, WILLIAM LAKE, ROBERT LANE, PETER LANGONE, SCOTT LARSEN, LT. JOSEPH LEAVEY, NEIL LEAVY, DANIEL LIBRETTI, CARLOS LILLO, ROBERT LINNANE, MICHAEL LYNCH, MICHAEL LYNCH, MICHAEL LYONS, PATRICK LYONS, JOSEPH MAFFEO, WILLIAM MAHONY, JOSEPH MALONEY, BATT. CHIEF MARCHBANKS JR., LT. CHARLES MARGIOTTA, KENNETH MARINO, JOHN MARSHALL, LT. PETER MARTIN, LT. PAUL MARTINI, JOSEPH MASCALI, KEITHROY MAYNARD, BRIAN MCALEESE, JOHN MCAVOY, THOMAS MACANN, LT. WILLIAM MCGINN, BATT. CHIEF WILLIAM MCGOVERN, DENNIS MCHUGH, ROBERT MCMAHON, ROBERT MCPADDEN, TERENCE MCSHANE, TIMOTHY MCSWEENEY, MARTIN MCWILLIAMS, RAY MEISENHEIMER, CHARLES MENDEZ, STEVE MERCADO, DOUGLAS MILLER, HENRY MILLER JR., ROBERT MINARA, THOMAS MINGIONE, LT. PAUL MITCHELL, CAPT. LOUIS MODAFFERI, LT. DENNIS MOJICA, MANUEL MOJICA, CARL MOLINARO, MICHAEL MONTESI, CAPT. THOMAS MOODY, BATT. CHIEF JOHN MORAN, VINCENT MORELLO, CHRISTOPHER MOZZILLO, RICHARD MULDOWNEY JR., MICHAEL MULLEN, DENNIS MULLIGAN, LT. RAYMOND MURPHY, LT. ROBERT NAGEL, JOHN NAPOLITANO, PETER NELSON, GERERD NEVINS, DENIS O'BERG, LT. DANIEL O'CALLAGHAN, DOUGLAS OELSCHLAGER, JOSEPH OGREN, LT. THOMAS O'HAGEN, SAMUAL OTICE, PATRICK O'KEEFE, CAPT. WILLIAM O'KEEFE, ERIC OLSEN, JEFFREY OLSEN, STEVEN OLSON, KEVIN O'ROURKE, MICHAEL OTTEN, JEFFREY PALAZZO, BATT. CHIEF ORIO PLAMER, FRANK PALOMBO, PAUL PANSINI, BATT. CHIEF JOHN PAOLILLO, JAMES PAPPAGEORGE, ROBERT PARRO, DURRELL PEARSALL, LT. GLENN PERRY, LT. PHILIP PETTI, LT. KEVIN PFEIFER, LT. KENNETH PHELAN, CHRISTOPHER PICKFORD, SHAWN POWELL, VINCENT PRINCIOTTA, KEVIN PRIOR, BATT. CHIEF RICHARD PRUNTY, LINCOLN QUAPPE, LT. MICHAEL QUILTY, RICARDO QUINN, LEONARD RAGAGLIA, MICHAEL RAGUSA, EDWARD RALL, ADAM, RAND, DONALD REGAN, LT. ROBERT REGENHARD, KEVIN REILLY, LT. VERNON RICHARD, JAMES RICHES, JOSEPH RIVELLI, MICHAEL ROBERTS, MICHAEL E. ROBERTS, ANTHONY RODRIGUEZ, MATTHEW ROGAN, KEITH ROMA, NICHOLAS ROSSOMANDO, PAUL RUBACK, STEPHAN RUSSELL, LT. MICHAEL RUSSO, BATT. CHIEF MATTHEW RYAN, THOMAS SABELLA, CHRISTOPHER SANTORA, JOHN SANTORE, GREGORY SAUCEDO, DENNIS SCAUSO, JOHN SCHARDT, BATT. CHIEF SCHEFFOLD, THOMAS SCHOALES, GERARD SCHRANG, GREGORY SIKORSKY, STEPHEN SILLER, STANLSY SMAGALA JR. KEVIN SMITH, LEON SMITH JR., ROBERT SPEAR JR., JOSEPH SPOR, BATT. CHIEF LAWRENCE STACK, CAPT. TIMOTHY STACKPOLE, GREGORY STAJK, JEFFREY STARK, BEMJAMIN SUAREZ, DANIEL SUHR, LT. CHRISTOPHER SULLIVAN, BRIAN SWEENEY, SEAN TALLON, ALLAN TARASIEWICZ, PAUL TEGTMEIER, JOHN TIERNEY, JOHN TIPPING III, HECTOR TIRADO JR. RICHARD VANHINE, PETER VEGA, LAWRENCE VELING, JOHN VIGIANO II, SERGIO VILLANUEVA, LAWRENCE VIRGILIO, LT. ROBERT WALLACE, JEFFREY WALZ, LT. MICHAEL WARCHOLA, CAPT. PATRICK WATERS, KENNETH WATSON, MICHAEL WEINBERG, DAVID WEISS, TIMOTHY WELTY, EUGENE WHELEN, EDWARD WHITE, MARK WHITFORD, LT. GLENN WILKINSON, BATT. CHIEF JOHN WILLIAMSON, CAPT. DAVID WOOLEY, RAYMOND YORK, 23 NYPD POLICE OFFICERS, 37 PORT AUTHORITY OFFICERS.

Michael B. Coleman
Mayor of The City of Columbus

Office of the Mayor

City Hall / 90 West Broad Street
Columbus, Ohio 43215-9014
614/645-7671
FAX 614/645-8955
TDD 614/645-6200

City Of Columbus Firefighters;

As Mayor of the City of Columbus, it is an honor to work with our Department of Public Safety and Division of Fire every day in service to our citizens.

For nearly two centuries, you have stood on the front lines of public safety, working to guarantee the health and well being of every Columbus resident, and this Division of Fire History Book is a testament to your success.

I believe that there is no higher calling than that of public service, and as each of you know, it takes more than just training and strength to be a firefighter, it takes a passion to do the right thing for others.

Every citizen owes a great debt of gratitude for the work of the Division, and the willingness of each firefighter to put the health and lives of Columbus families before their own.

Congratulations and thank you for everything you do to make this a great city for our families, for businesses and for the future.

We are grateful and proud.

Sincerely,

Michael B. Coleman
Mayor

MITCHELL J. BROWN
CITY OF COLUMBUS
SAFETY DIRECTOR

City of Columbus
Department of Public Safety

50 W. Gay Street, 2nd Floor
Columbus, Ohio 43215-9035
(614) 645-8210 FAX 645-8268

City of Columbus Firefighters:

Third Edition of Division of Fire History Book
Letter from Director Brown

As Safety Director for this great city, please let me extend a measure of gratitude and appreciation to each and every fire fighter for putting your lives on the line to protect our citizens.

The Division of Fire's history book provides a good opportunity to reflect on nearly two hundred years of outstanding fire and emergency medical service to the central Ohio community. The tradition to protect and serve has been carried on through many generations of men and women who put the citizens' safety before their own.

Columbus is fortunate at have one of the very best Fire Divisions in the country.
From becoming the first major U.S. city to be equipped with a medic in every fire station to participating in the first-ever high-rise training, our fire fighters represent the best kind of public servants.

We are a 21st century city that continues to grow and change for the better. History has shown that our fire fighters are up to the challenge—past, present and future!

Congratulations to all of you on your contributions to our Fire Division's rich tradition.

Sincerely,

Mitchell J. Brown
Director

COLUMBUS CITY COUNCIL

CITY COUNCIL PRESIDENT
MATTHEW D. HABASH

MICHAEL C. MENTEL

KEVIN L. BOYCE

MARYELLEN O'SHAUGHNESSY

CHARLETA B. TAVARES

RICHARD W. SENSENBRENNER

JENNETTE B. BRADLEY

DIVISION OF FIRE
NED PETTUS SR., FIRE CHIEF
3675 PARSONS AVENUE
COLUMBUS, OHIO 43207-4054

To the Members of the Columbus Division of Fire:

As I write this in the Summer of 2002, the Columbus Division of Fire is 180 years from its beginning as a volunteer fire department. We have come a long way. Today, we are the 15th largest fire department in the country, and in many respects the nation's leader.

We are the only metropolitan fire department that staffs every engine as a paramedic engine, has a fully staffed paramedic-level ambulance in every fire station, and trains ever Division member as an EMT-B. We have the largest non-military Bomb Squad in the country. Both our Bomb Squad and Hazardous Materials Team have received the highest training available and employ the most advanced technology.

Our training staff is responsible for all of the ongoing and initial training of our 1,500 firefighters and our 600 paramedics. They conducted live fire training in a high rise structure last year, which drew observers from around the country and resulted in a published article in *Fire Engineering*. Our recently developed technical rescue training is comparable to any program in the country. We contribute several members to Ohio's only federal Urban Search and Rescue team, Task Force 1, which responded to the World Trade Center incidents in New York City on September 11, 2001.

The Columbus Division of Fire also reaches out into the community with fire prevention and education. We have a Juvenile Firesetter Program which receives many referrals from Juvenile Court and offers counseling to hundreds of children each year. We teach CPR in the Columbus Public Schools. We have a Fire Fighters Against Drugs program which has produced several unique tutoring and mentoring programs. The Community Relations Office, responsible for much of this public outreach, coordinated nearly 900 fire safety programs and presentations last year.

As I am sure it was true nearly 200 years ago, it is the men and women of the Columbus Division of Fire, both uniform and non-uniform, who make ours a great fire department. Their integrity, dedication, and professionalism set them apart from all others. May this history book serve as a reminder to future generations of the exceptional people who make this department what it is today.

I am personally very thankful for the opportunity God has given me to serve as their Fire Chief, and I will forever be proud to have been a member of the best fire department in the world.

Sincerely,

Ned Pettus, Jr.
Fire Chief

NED PETTUS SR.
FIRE CHIEF

COLUMBUS FIRE FIGHTERS UNION LOCAL 67

As the President of our great Local, it is an honor to serve the Professional Fire Fighters of IAFF Local 67.

The men and women of the Columbus Division of Fire who have dedicated their lives protecting the citizens of Columbus are contained within the pages of this history book. I hope you enjoy this history book and on behalf of the members of Local 67 IAFF, I would like to personally thank all the members who have worked so hard putting this history book together.

In closing, your Local will continue to keep you protected when you are fulfilling the responsibility of answering the call. Whether it is Fire or EMS, the Proud Professional Union Fire Fighters of the Columbus Division of Fire are second to none.

Fraternally,

Kevin Harr
President
Local 67, IAFF

COLUMBUS FIRE FIGHTERS UNION LOCAL 67

As the newest President of the Columbus Fire Fighter's Union, I am honored to be given the opportunity to speak for the members of this great Local. I would be remiss if I did not publicly acknowledge the work of the great group of past presidents of Local 67.

The pages within this book represent the best our members have to offer…their lives. As we are all aware, firefighting is not a career, it is a livelihood. And our members put forth their best efforts on a daily basis to meet the needs of the Citizens of Columbus and its visitors. Our members not only fight fires as aggressively as any in the country, they are pioneers in the delivery of Emergency Medical Services, they perform hazardous materials mitigation, they perform complex technical rescues, they answer and appropriately handle 911 calls from anxious citizens, and they adapt to almost any emergency situation put before them. They do all this while maintaining a professional, polite and calm demeanor.

This book has been put together by a group of members who have worked tirelessly to portray our members in the proudest possible light. Thank you to all of you on behalf of the rest of us, we do appreciate your documentation of our lives.

Fraternally,

Jack Reall, President
Columbus Fire Fighter's Union
IAFF Local 67

1380 Dublin Road • Suite 103 • Columbus, Ohio 43215 • 614-481-8900 • Fax: 481-7400

Fire Chiefs Of CFD

C. H. Ridgeway
1855-1860

John Miller
1860-1863

I. H. Marrow
1863-1868

Henry Heinmiller
1869-1880, 1890-1899

D. D. Tresnenrider
1880-1885, 1886-1890

Charles Bryson
1885-1886

Charles J. Lauer
1899-1915

Jenkins Daniels
1915-1926

A. E. "Dude" Nice
1926-1933

Willis Hunt
1933

Edward P. Welch
1933-1942, 1944-1947

Clarence Ogborn
1942-1944, 1948

Walter G. Strickfaden
1948-1966

J. C. O'Connor
1966

Glenn Barr
1966-1971

Raymond R. Fadley
1971-1983

Donald E. Werner Jr.
1983-1991

Harmon J. Dutko
1991-1997

Stephen K. Woltz
1997-2002

Ned Pettus, Sr.
2002-

Columbus Division of Fire Rank

Fire Chief

Deputy Chief

Assistant Chief

Lieutenant

Captain

Battalion Chief

Firefighter

Fire Inspector

Fire Investigator

Fire Chaplain

INTRODUCTION
HISTORY OF THE COLUMBUS DIVISION OF FIRE

The first serious fire in Columbus occurred in 1822, destroying eight buildings. Up to this time there was no organized fire department or fire fighting equipment available to the residents of Columbus. The Town Council directed the Mayor to draft residents to form a volunteer fire brigade. The fire brigade would consist of twelve men to man a ladder company, fifteen men to form a hook and axe company, and twelve men to guard property. All other men between the ages of 15 and 50 were to form a bucket brigade at any fire. To equip the new volunteer fire companies, money was appropriated to buy six ladders, four axes and two hooks. No provision was made to purchase fire buckets. Instead, all property owners were required to have ten-quart leather buckets on hand or be subject to a fine. The Town Council also appointed a Supreme Director to take charge at all fires and the Town Marshall was made responsible for ringing the fire alarm bell. This was the beginning of the Columbus Fire Department, over 180 years ago.

In 1823 the Council purchased Columbus' first hand-pumped fire engine, called the Tub. At a fire the bucket brigade would pour water into the hand-operated force pump while several men would pump the water from the engine into a fire hose. This stream of hand-pumped water would then be forced out of a nozzle and aimed at the fire by a hose crew at the scene of the fire. The Tub was in service for twelve years and was effectively used to put out a fire at the penitentiary. In 1824 an engine house was built on the Public Square, east of the State House, to house the hand engine.

Fire prevention efforts began in 1831 when Council passed an ordinance requiring inspection of all flues and chimneys and imposed a five dollar fine on anyone whose property had a dirty or unsafe chimney. In the same ordinance, Council offered to pay five dollars to the first fireman to arrive at the engine house in the event of an alarm, four dollars to the second man and three dollars to the third. If two or three men arrived at the same time, they were to decide by lot who was first. No one was paid for a false alarm.

Columbus was incorporated into a City in 1834, with a population of about three thousand residents. The new City Council passed an ordinance on June 11, 1835 creating a company of fire guards, a protection and salvage company, a hook and ladder company, an engine company, a hose company and a company of fire wardens. On July 25, $1,000 was appropriated to build a new engine house. On August 25, Council allocated money to build five cisterns (underground water storage tanks used for fire fighting), dig four wells equipped with pumps, and to connect the wells to the cisterns with piping to keep them full.

On November 13, 1835, two new hand engines, the Niagra and the Constitution, replaced the Tub purchased in 1823. These hand engines were capable of drafting water out of the new cisterns, thus eliminating the need for a bucket brigade. As the city grew, new cisterns were added to cover the new areas. Over the next twenty years the City bought additional hand engines, including the Scioto, Franklin, Old Zack, Eagle and Fame. The hook and ladder company was called the Salamander H&L Company, and the hose companies were called the Relief, Phoenix and Hornet.

Basic fire fighting equipment and methods changed very little during the following years and the volunteer fire department did what it could with the equipment available. Occasional disasters brought brief periods of public interest in the volunteer fire department and it went through cycles of growth and decline. No record remains of the volunteers' service with the exception of the fires they could not put out. One example is a fire that destroyed William Neal's steam sawmill and 40,000 board feet of new lumber in August 1839. Between 1840 and 1850, a tannery, a brewery, a large commercial building and several tenement houses burned down. In 1852 the State House was almost totally destroyed by fire, and a sash factory was destroyed in 1855.

In 1852, the city council of Cincinnati witnessed a public experiment of a steam fire engine. They contracted to purchase the fire engine and it was placed in service under a company organized and put under pay by the city. Thus the first paid Fire Company to operate with steam was brought into existence, the first of the kind in this age or country. In 1853 their entire fire department was changed from hand to steam. It was a great step forward for the benefit of the Queen City and the whole country.

Columbus leaders visited Cincinnati and were impressed with the steam fire engines. In 1854 they reported in favor of purchasing a steam fire engine for Columbus. The change from the old to the new system was not made without difficulties. It needed firmness and determination to stem the tide of opposition. These qualities were found in the chairman of the standing committee on the fire department, Luther Donaldson, who took the matter in hand. Through his determined efforts Columbus was the fourth city in the country to adopt a steam and paid fire department, following Cincinnati, New Orleans and Boston.

In September of 1855 the fire department committee traveled to Cincinnati to witness the trial of the new steamer, named Columbus. During the trial the engine burst a steam pipe and Columbus citizens were disappointed to not receive their engine at the appointed time.

In October of 1855 a new fire ordinance was adopted which included the election of C.M. Ridgway as Engineer to take charge of the new engine when it arrived. Mr. J. C. Kenyon was elected Chief Engineer of the Fire Department Committee, which oversaw the operation of the fire department. This arrangement created antagonism between the firemen and the "political" committee. After a very heated election for one Chief Engineer, C. M. Ridgway was elected Chief Engineer on the one hundred seventieth ballot.

On October 2, 1855, the long looked-for engine arrived accompanied by its builder, Mr. Latta. There were numerous celebrations and the $6,000 steamer was placed in the recently built engine house on Third Street.

The horses required to pull this heavy piece of machinery are what necessitated a "paid" fire crew. The horses required constant attention in their feeding, care and training. The new complex steam machinery also required regular maintenance, and the boilers were frequently pre-heated in the engine house to speed up pumping response time.

On May 11, 1856, another new ordinance for the reorganization of the fire department was passed, which vested its control in the Fire Committee. Chief Engineer Ridgway was succeeded by Mr. Trowbridge.

November 6, 1860 marked a turning point in the history of the Columbus Fire Department. The Neil House Hotel fire was the worst fire in the city's history and demonstrated the inadequacy of the existing organization and equipment. Fighting a fire in the old wood frame hotel would have been difficult for a modern fire department using the latest equipment and techniques. At the time, however, Columbus' only steamer was in the shop for extensive repair work. The still mostly volunteer fire department faced a hopeless task against the city's worst fire, using two hand engines pumping from cisterns.

As a result of this fire, City Council appointed a special committee to report on the condition of the fire department and its inadequacy. On November 19, 1860, two weeks after the disaster, the committee reported that the two hand engines were in good condition and the steamer needed extensive repairs. Being overly cautious on buying a new steamer, the council decided to buy three new hand engines. At the same time, they called in H. C. Silsby to demonstrate one of his new rotary steam fire engines. After seeing the demonstration the city ordered two of the engines. The order for the three hand engines was cancelled and it was decided to scrap the old steam engine, which was at this time was named the Firefly.

The first steam engine had created bitter dissention among the volunteer hand engine companies. One of the hand engine companies disbanded in protest before the first steamer even arrived. Antagonism between the paid steam engine company and the volunteer companies continued to grow. Volunteer fire companies were formed, disbanded and reorganized over the next few years, and the fire department itself was reorganized several times.

The new steamers built by Silsby cost half as much as the original Latta engine purchased in 1855, and were much more dependable and efficient. The first two were delivered in 1861 and were named the Ben Blake and Joseph Ridgway, after two prominent council members. A third Silsby steamer went into service in 1863 and was named the John Miller. Additional equipment was needed to support the new steamers. A hose wagon was needed to supply hose from the steamer to the fire; larger hook and ladders were needed for the taller buildings; and the steamers needed coal wagons to supply coal once they were at the scene of the fire. All of this equipment required more horses and more men. Paid firemen, engineers and drivers now manned the steamers and additional equipment, living in the engine houses to take care of the horses and equipment.

On November 26, 1860, an ordinance created the office of Chief Engineer, placing the fire department under control of one head, and looking to the interest of the whole community. Selected by unanimous vote, banker John Miller undertook the task of organizing and bringing the new department into working order. He had police authority to arrest disobedient members, and a salary of $600 per year. Under his administration the third steamer was purchased. After serving as Chief Engineer for three years, he tendered his resignation to the council. The Columbus steam fire department had met the expectations of its early friends. The superiority of the steam system was now a fixed fact; its superiority over muscular power had been demonstrated.

Isaac Marrow became the Chief Engineer in November 1863. The department consisted of three Silsby steamers, three engineers, three firemen, three hosemen, three drivers and six extra men who were paid two dollars each time they worked at a fire. He organized the police patrolmen into a fire guard and divided the city into five districts with the policemen designated to man a bell tower in case of fire. They would strike the bell a designated number of rings, which corresponded, to the district in which the fire was located. In 1865, he recommended a fire telegraph alarm system and repeated the recommendation in his next two annual reports. In February, 1868, Council finally appropriated $4,500 for a Gamewell Telegraph System.

Chief Marrow retired six months later, succeeded by William Huffman who served from 1868 to 1869. The small, but well organized, department now consisted of three engineers, three firemen, three engine drivers, three hosemen, two truckmen, a superintendent of fire telegraph, four steamers, four hose wagons and one hook and ladder. It served to protect a population of 25,000 people. Henry Heinmiller was appointed Chief Engineer in April 1869 and served until 1880.

The first written fire records of the Columbus Fire Department covered the nine years between 1863 and 1872. Several fires believed to be the work of arsonists occurred in rapid succession in 1863, along with nine other major fires during this period. A major fire occurred in 1865, which destroyed two carriage factories. Columbus was the capital of carriage building in the Midwest during this time. In 1867 a furniture company, five stores and a penitentiary shop were destroyed.

On October 18, 1868, a fire started in the east wing of the Insane Asylum on East Broad Street. The fire spread rapidly through the old wood frame structure, and several inmates were unable to escape from the four hundred forty-room building before it was destroyed. The building, valued at $200,000 at the time, was 370 feet long and 218 feet deep.

The first Columbus Firefighter to be killed in the line of duty was Fireman Mark Newman. He was killed by falling walls while fighting a fire at the Columbus Woolen Mills in 1870. As of this writing there have been over 40 Columbus Firefighters killed in the line of duty.

In November 1872, a horse disease swept the country and Columbus' horses were struck on November 27th. This epidemic lasted nineteen days, during which volunteer companies were organized to pull the apparatus to and from the fires.

A new engine house for the city was built in 1874, but no new steamers would be purchased until 1890. The city fathers believed that the new city water system made the steam engines unnecessary since hose lines could be laid directly from the new hydrants to supply fire streams at a fire. Chief Heinmiller pointed out that the steamers could supply more water at higher pressures, but he was ordered to take them out of service and use them only when needed. By 1876, hose wagons began responding to fire alarms without the steamers. Although the steamers were fired up once a week, they slowly deteriorated while in storage. Three steamers were left with only one in good condition by 1882.

In late 1874, the department's first chemical engine was purchased to reduce the damage caused by water at a fire. It was followed by a combination chemical engine and salvage wagon, which was donated by the Board of Underwriters. The city furnished two men for it with one serving as driver and the other as hose man. The Board of Underwriters furnished ten men who were paid only when they did salvage work at a fire.

The city was turned into a state of panic by a string of fires set by arsonists between March 1 and March 11, 1879. The first fire occurred March 1st at the County Court House where many county records were destroyed. Immediately following this incident, five more fires were set and two buildings were completely destroyed between the hours of 6:00 p.m. and midnight. From this day on until March 11th, two to five fires were set every night. The fire department managed to control the fires, saving the city from being destroyed. Martial law was declared during this time and the Fourteenth Regiment was called to duty to watch over the city, which ended the burning.

After the department's battle with the arsonists, a political conflict arose in which Chief Heinmiller was removed from his office. D. D. Tresenrider was appointed as replacement on September 6, 1880. The Mayor subsequently suspended him from office on March 2, 1885. City Council refused to concur with the Mayor's decision. The case was taken to the Supreme Court, which ruled in favor of Council. The Mayor next appointed Charles Bryson and Council again refused to confirm the appointment. Bryson remained in the position until the Supreme Court also ruled him out. The Mayor continued to attempt to replace Tresenrider against City Council's wishes. City Council finally obtained an injunction restraining the Mayor from interfering with the supervision of the fire department and Chief Tresenrider was reinstated.

As the city continued to grow, water mains were extended farther and farther from their source. At first, hydrant pressure was sufficient for supplying fire streams, but after years of extending the mains, the pumping plant could no longer supply adequate pressure for fire streams. Chief Heinmiller's warning to not rely on hydrant pressure proved to be well founded.

The department was forced to return to the use of steamers, which proved to be a costly conversion. The two reserve steamers remaining from the 1870's were in too poor condition to use. In 1890, two new Ahrens steamers were purchased and placed in service at Engine Houses 2 and 4. Six additional Ahrens steamers were purchased later that year. Two engine houses built during the 1880's had to be completely rebuilt because they were to small to accommodate the steamers.

In 1890, the legislature passed a bill reorganizing the city government and created a Board of Public Works to be elected by the people after the first year. Henry Heinmiller was appointed as Superintendent of the Fire Department as one of the first appointments made by the Board. During the next ten years, seven new engine houses were built and six were rebuilt to accommodate the steamers and space for other new apparatus. The entire fire alarm system was completely modernized under Heinmiller. The department grew from sixty-five men to a force of over one hundred-fifty men with an additional twenty-five substitutes.

During Chief Heinmiller's second decade as Chief other important changes were instituted. Firemen worked seven days a week in 1890 and were given time off for meals at home, twelve hours off duty per week and seven days annual vacation. On May 25, 1896, Council increased the annual vacation to twelve days. Then the annual vacation was removed on December 12, 1897, and the firemen were given twenty-four hours off per week. On June 24, 1901, Council gave the firemen ten days vacation while retaining their work schedule of six days per week.

Charles J. Lauer succeeded Heinmiller as Chief in 1899 and continued to make many improvements. It was during this time that the department grew internally. Chief Lauer established an internal maintenance system for the department. Apparatus no longer had to be sent from the city for repair, nor did the engine houses have to wait to be repaired or repainted. Chief Lauer was like a father to his men, with their problems being his problems. A strong bond grew between them and on January 1, 1900, the men of Engine House #1 pooled their funds and purchased a large gold badge for him in appreciation of his service.

The transition to motorized equipment began under Chief Lauer's administration. The last engine house built to house horses was Engine House #16, built in 1908. In 1909 an automobile was purchased for the Chief, and in the following year autos were purchased for two more chiefs. Two 8-cylinder Seagrave tractors were purchased in 1913 and replaced horses on Engine 1, a 1250 gpm Continental steamer, and Ladder 1, a Seagrave 85' spring raised aerial ladder. Five more horse drawn apparatus were motorized over the next year. The city's first gasoline powered pumper, made by Seagrave, was placed in service in 1912. It was stationed at new Engine House #17, the first station built without a barn for horses.

The first comparison speed tests of motorized equipment took place on February 17, 1913. These tests took place on East Broad Street and Fourth Street. The horse drawn apparatus ran the course first, and then the motorized apparatus covered the same course immediately afterward. The results were as follows:

One-mile run:
Horse drawn engine   3 minutes 38 seconds
Steam engine with tractor   2 minutes 40 seconds

Two-mile run:
Horse drawn engine   7 minutes 25 seconds
Steam engine with tractor   4 minutes 57 seconds

Three-mile run:
Horse-drawn engine   11 minutes 45 seconds
Steam engine with tractor   7 minutes

The motorized vehicles were the clear winners and spelled the demise of horses in the Columbus Fire Department.

Chief Charles J. Lauer passed away on September 10, 1915, after a short illness. Assistant Chief Jenkins Daniels was temporarily appointed Chief until a Civil Service test could be conducted. After successfully passing the test, he was appointed Chief on October 9, 1915. He was the first Chief to come up through the ranks. Chief Daniels took over a department in the middle of a change from nineteenth-century steamers to twentieth-century gasoline engines. The change was completed on December 27, 1919 when the department's last horses were retired from Engine House #16 at Chestnut and N. Fourth Street.

The end of the horse drawn era was not the only notable event that took place in 1919. Thirty-three major fires occurred between 1890 and 1920, with the most disastrous fire occurring at midnight on May 5, 1919. A newspaper account written several years after the fire described it as a scene of horror when the fire department arrived. The Philadelphia Block was a large six-story wood frame tenement building at Broad and Front Streets. Men, women and children, trapped in their beds by the rapidly spreading smoke and flames, were screaming for help. The first companies to arrive concentrated all their efforts on saving as many lives as possible. Ten people were rescued from ladders hastily thrown up to windows, and many more people jumped into life nets. Some of the screaming victims jumped to their deaths instead of dying in the flames. Ten people died in this fire because of a swinging gas light, which was forbidden by the fire code, when it ignited a wall in a second floor bathroom. The fire spread so quickly that the iron fire escapes were too hot to use within a very short time. One woman was found dead in her bath. The disaster enabled the fire department to eliminate many similar conditions in other buildings over the next few years to help prevent a recurrence of the tragedy.

The department consisted of 355 men by 1921. In his first Annual Report, Chief Daniels recommended more time off for his men and continued to make that recommendation every year. Council eventually changed the work schedule, giving every fireman one-day off after seventy-two hours of work. This doubled their time off, but they were still working one hundred-twenty hours a week. The two-platoon system was finally set up in 1921 after a long and hard struggle with the city fathers. The two-platoon system greatly increased the morale and efficiency of the fire department and an extra platoon of men was now available in case of an emergency.

The Annual Report for 1926 by Chief Nice listed fifty-eight pieces of motorized apparatus, including eleven 1000 gpm Seagrave pumpers, one Seagrave-Gorman pumper, seven smaller engines, four 85 foot aerial ladder trucks and five service ladder trucks. All the trucks were equipped with Burrell All-Service breathing masks. The aerial ladders carried two masks and the service ladder trucks carried one. The city's first high-rise building, now called the Leveque Tower at Broad and Front Street, presented Chief Nice with a new fire fighting problem in 1927. Engine House #18 opened this same year and with it came a new 750 gpm Seagrave engine. This was the first engine in the department to have a booster tank and a one-inch hose line on a reel. Station 19 was built in 1930 and would be the last engine house built in Columbus for another 20 years.

The worst fire disaster in the city's history occurred at the Ohio State Penitentiary on April 21, 1930. A set fire, intended to cover an escape attempt, started too early and caught the prisoners still in their cells. 322 convicts were killed. This fire still remains the worst fire in Columbus' history.

By 1931 the department had eleven fewer men than in 1926. The city government was running in the red and the situation worsened. In February 1936, the taxpayers defeated a 3-mill fire levy, which resulted in a reduction in pensions. The next day, falling walls at the Odd Fellows Temple fire killed five firefighters, and two men were pensioned for disability. One hundred eighty-seven men were furloughed in March 1936, closing Engine Houses 3, 4, 5, 6, 11, 12, 13, 17 and 19. Two of these houses were not reopened until the 1950's. Twenty men returned to duty in one week and the rest returned to duty on June 10, 1936, after a new fire levy was passed.

Chief Nice retired because of a physical disability on January 1, 1933. Mayor Worley appointed Battalion Chief Willis B. Hunt to the position of Provisional Chief. On February 12, 1933, while he was preparing for the Chief's examination, Chief Hunt passed away a month and four days after his provisional appointment. Assistant Chief Clarence Ogborn was then appointed Provisional Chief in place of Hunt until a civil service test was conducted. Because of the lack of applicants in the Chiefs' ranks, the test for Chief was opened to members with the rank of Captain. As a result of the testing process, Captain E. P. Welch was appointed to the position of Fire Chief.

When Chief Welch was appointed in 1933, the fire department was short thirty firemen. It was also noted that there were no longer any black firefighters in the department. The last colored Chemical Company was disbanded in 1913. Mayor Worley instructed that a civil service test be given and that black applicants be especially selected from the resulting list. Upon completion of their training, the black firefighters were to be assigned to Station 8 at 20th Street and Mt. Vernon Avenue. The black firefighters remained at this station, even after they were promoted, until 1953 when the fire department integrated the firefighters into other stations around the city. Even with these appointments, the total manpower of the department continued to decline, and in 1936, the fire department had fifty less firemen than it had in 1930, and the situation would not improve until 1941.

These were lean years for every department of the municipal government and for the fire department. However, significant changes occurred even during the Depression years. Engine companies became more versatile as equipment was modernized. By 1935, fifteen engine companies had one-inch hose lines and water tanks on the trucks. By 1937 every first-line pumper had a one-inch booster line. Columbus was one of the first cities in the United States to use 1 1/2 inch hose lines. Engines 11 and 17 were equipped with 11/2-inch hand lines in 1935, and by 1940 every engine company carried it. Engine companies now had much more maneuverability for fighting fires inside a building in comparison to using 21/2 inch hose lines.

One of the first emergency squads in the country went into service in Columbus in 1934 at Engine House #6. It was a 1927 Seagrave hose wagon converted into an emergency squad, initially designed to take care of injured firefighters. Radios were being installed in Chiefs' cars, and in 1935 four new Chiefs' cars were purchased with radios. Radios were also being installed in fire apparatus with enclosed cabs. A public address system was installed in all engine houses in 1938. A new cross-index street card system was compiled by a W.P.A. project and put to use in the Fire Alarm Office. This provided quicker and more accurate assignment of fire apparatus.

One hundred sixty-eight fires occurred during the Depression decade, including thirty-two third alarm fires and six fourth-alarm fires. One of these was on November 16, 1937, at the Woolworth 5 & 10 store. Three alarms and all extra companies were called to the fire, which destroyed two buildings. Firemen fought the fire for more than forty-two hours in freezing weather. The fire companies used 2,400 gallons of gasoline operating the apparatus while working at this fire.

Between 1940 and 1943, during World War II, the fire department bought eleven pumpers and three ladder trucks while fire apparatus was still available. Sixty-one firemen were hired in 1941 to help replace those who left for military duty. Chief Welch received a commission as a Captain in the U.S. Army in 1942 and obtained a leave of absence from the fire department. Clarence Ogborn was appointed Chief during his absence. By 1944, fifty Columbus firemen were in the Armed Forces. Through disabilities and retirements, the department had eighty firemen less than it had in 1941. Chief Welch and thirty-four firemen returned from the military in 1945.

Chief Welch died suddenly of a heart attack on February 27, 1947, and Clarence Ogborn was appointed Chief of the Department. He retired the following year after thirty-eight years of service.

In the November election of 1947, the citizens of Columbus voted the fire department a forty-hour workweek. Prior to this, fire personnel worked every other twenty-four hour shift, with an extra day off every other week, for a total of seventy-two hours a week. The department lacked the manpower to implement the newly voted work schedule without having to take four pump companies and three truck companies out of service. As the schedule was implemented, the day was divided into three shifts. The first shift did the routine work around the Engine House, the second shift did building inspections, and the third shift checked hydrants after midnight. Dissatisfaction with the new work schedule was widespread and the morale of the fire department disintegrated. Seven firemen resigned, and twenty-one retired, include nine officers.

Fire union negotiators offered that firemen would work an extra sixteen hours per week if the city would adopt a three-platoon system. This proposed work schedule would ease the manpower shortage and increase the efficiency of the fire department by simplifying the work schedule and improving morale among the men. Most of the firemen signed a petition, which threatened mass resignations unless the work schedule was changed. The Mayor ignored the threat and implied that the firemen were not irreplaceable. The firemen went to the people of the city asking for a Charter Amendment to change the work schedule. The Charter Amendment passed in November 1948, and established the existing three-platoon system. Morale greatly improved with the adoption of the fifty-six hour, three-platoon system.

On May 16, 1948, Walter Strickfadden was appointed Fire Chief. The department now had thirty first-line and back-up triple-combination pumpers; one aerial ladder truck with a 750-gpm pump called a quint; nine ladder trucks, twelve chiefs' cars and five emergency squad cars.

Since no new Engine Houses had been built since 1930, several were now needed. Two new houses (20, 21) opened in 1951 with an additional two more (22, 23) within the next two years to protect the new post-war housing developments. Four more stations were added during the second half of the decade as the city continued to grow.

Eight new engines, two ladder trucks, and a quad with a 65-foot ladder and 750-gpm pump were purchased between 1948 and 1953. The department had several self-contained air masks in 1949 and continued to buy more of them during the early fifties. By this time, fog nozzles had become an important tool in fighting structure fires. The Navy had developed the combination fog nozzle for fighting fires on ships during World War II. The nozzle proved to be very versatile and appeared in 11/2-inch hose beds of several engine companies after the war. (It has been said these nozzles were borrowed from the Navy by returning servicemen who saw their potential.) By the late fifties, all engine companies in the city were equipped with one inch and one and a half-inch combination fog nozzles. The combination of the new style nozzle, more maneuverable 11/2 inch hose and air masks made inside fire fighting much more effective.

In 1959, the department consisted of 121 officers and 496 firefighters. Equipment consisted of twenty-seven pumpers, one quad, one turret wagon, nine aerial ladder trucks, one fire squad, four emergency squads, eight chiefs' cars and sixty-three other pieces of equipment.

One hundred eighty-nine major fires occurred during the fifties, including thirty-two three-alarm fires and two four-alarm fires. These include the Doddington Lumber Yard and 40 West Gay Street in 1952; Kauffman-Lattimer, General Laundry and North Columbus Lumber Company in 1954; Rite Rug Company, Reebs Restaurant and 483 Neilston in 1955; the O.S.U. Armory and Rich and High Street in 1958; and Lord Hall in 1959.

Chief Strickfadden retired in 1966, after sixty years in the fire service. His years of service saw the department grow from 135 firefighters to 525, and from 47 officers to 155. During his eighteen years as Chief, ten new engine houses were built and the department grew by 251 men. During his last year in the department, a Mack diesel pumper was purchased. It would be the first of the diesel motors that would gradually replace the gasoline engines in use since 1912.

Upon the retirement of Chief Strickfadden on August 29, 1966, Assistant Chief J.C. O'Connor was appointed Provisional Chief. Chief O'Connor held this position until his service retirement on December 31, 1966. Glenn Barr served as Chief for the next four and a half years, during which time four new engine houses were built; twelve diesel fire apparatus were purchased; and several of the V-12 gas engines in the old Seagrave engines and ladders were replaced with diesel engines. The new diesel apparatus included six GMC engines, three Mack-Thibault 100-foot aerial ladders, and three GMC tractors, which replaced Seagrave tractors on 85-foot aerial ladder trucks.

Race riots tore the city apart during June 1969, and numerous fires were set at one time. In many cities, firefighters had bricks and stones thrown at them when they tried to extinguish the fires. In an attempt to protect the firefighters and equipment responding into the riot areas, task forces of apparatus were formed. In case of a fire, the companies that composed the task force would meet at a predetermined place outside the riot area. They would then respond into the riot area together. This provided more protection for the firefighter, rather than having companies responding individually into the riot-torn area.

Raymond Fadley was appointed Chief on May 19, 1971. During the next five years he expanded the Emergency Medical Service. The Heartmobile, a mobile coronary care unit, was created from a federal grant in 1969, and grew to four 'Medic' units under Chief Fadley's administration. The growth of the Emergency Medical Service can also be attributed to the foresight and guidance of Dr. James V. Warren, M.D., Professor and Chairman of the Department of Medicine, Ohio State University Hospital. The Emergency Medical Service was further expanded with the addition of four heavy rescue units in 1973.

The first engine to have a 1000-gallon booster tank was put into service at Engine House #1 in 1972. On March 1, 1973, another first for the department occurred when the division turned to the use of a different kind of fire hose. This new hose has a jacket made from a type of plastic and lightweight 'SnapTite/Storz Couplings'. One thousand feet each of 5 inch and 3 inch hose, and two, two-hundred foot beds of 2 inch hose were placed on Engine 3 for testing on actual fire grounds. The larger diameter hose proved to be a definite asset for supplying our engines and is now standard equipment on all new apparatus. Revenue sharing money was used to buy 5 Squrts in 1974. The Squrt has a 54-foot articulating boom with a nozzle that adjusts from 350 gpm to 1000 gpm. These units were mounted on a GMC truck chassis powered by a V-6 diesel engine. The operator controls the boom, the direction of the nozzle and the stream pattern from a control panel above the rear running board. The Squrt functions as a water tower and as a hose wagon; much like the two separate vehicles in the early 1900's, and does both jobs better.

The Division was reorganized into five Bureaus early in 1974, with each Bureau headed by an Assistant Chief. This assignment placed a strong administrative head over each of the five major functions of the Division of Fire.

According to Chief Fadley, 'Great strides were made in 1975 regarding the CORES program (Central Ohio Regional Emergency Services).' It was expected that, in 1976, all Franklin County fire departments would become members of the organization and participate in Automatic Response, where the closest fire department would respond to a fire regardless of the political jurisdiction. Automatic Response not only improved service to the citizens of the jurisdictions, but it also resulted in insurance premium reductions.

In 1976, the Columbus Division of Fire consisted of 836 members, 180 pieces of apparatus, 25 engine houses, and an administrative and training complex. Expenditures for 1975 totaled $18,665,842.

Chief Fadley retired on December 31, 1983 and Chief Don Werner took over the reins of the Division of Fire. Considered a 'Firefighters' Chief', he personally knew each and every firefighter by name and face. Following the tradition of Chief Lauer, he looked out for his men. He could be found at the firehouses 'talking fire' with the crew.

Chief Werner retired on May 11, 1991. His Executive Office, Chief Harmon Dutko, took over the fire department and increased its size and strength. During this period of time, the City of Columbus was purchasing large areas of land and incorporating them into the city. This led the fire department into further growth as this land was developed. Stations 30, 31, 32 and 33 were built to cover these rapidly expanding areas. In 1995 the Division moved all of its training and administrative functions to a new complex located on Parsons Avenue. The old Wherle High School complex was purchased and converted into a state-of-the-art training complex and administrative bureau.

Chief Dutko retired on March 8, 1997, and his Executive Officer, Chief Stephen K. Woltz, was appointed Chief. In 1997, Chief Woltz oversaw the conversion of our EMS system from BLS and ALS units, to all Advanced Life Support units. Every engine house in the City has an Advanced Life Support engine and medic in it, totaling 66 ALS vehicles in Columbus.

In the year 2002, 180 years since the founding of the Columbus Division of Fire, the department consists of the following firefighters and equipment. The authorized (2001) uniformed firefighter strength is 1575 men and women. There are 33 engines, 9 aerial platform ladders and 6 tillered aerial ladders, 31 ALS Medics, 5 Heavy Rescues, 1 HazMat vehicle, 1 Bomb Disposal Unit, 7 Battalion Chiefs, 7 EMS Supervisors, and numerous maintenance and support vehicles. There are 31 stations (two with double engines), with 33 numbered engines. Station 34 will soon be built and plans are in the works for stations 35 and 36. The annual budget for the year 2001 was $130,592,000. In 2002, Chief Ned Pettus was sworn in as new Chief of Columbus Division of Fire.

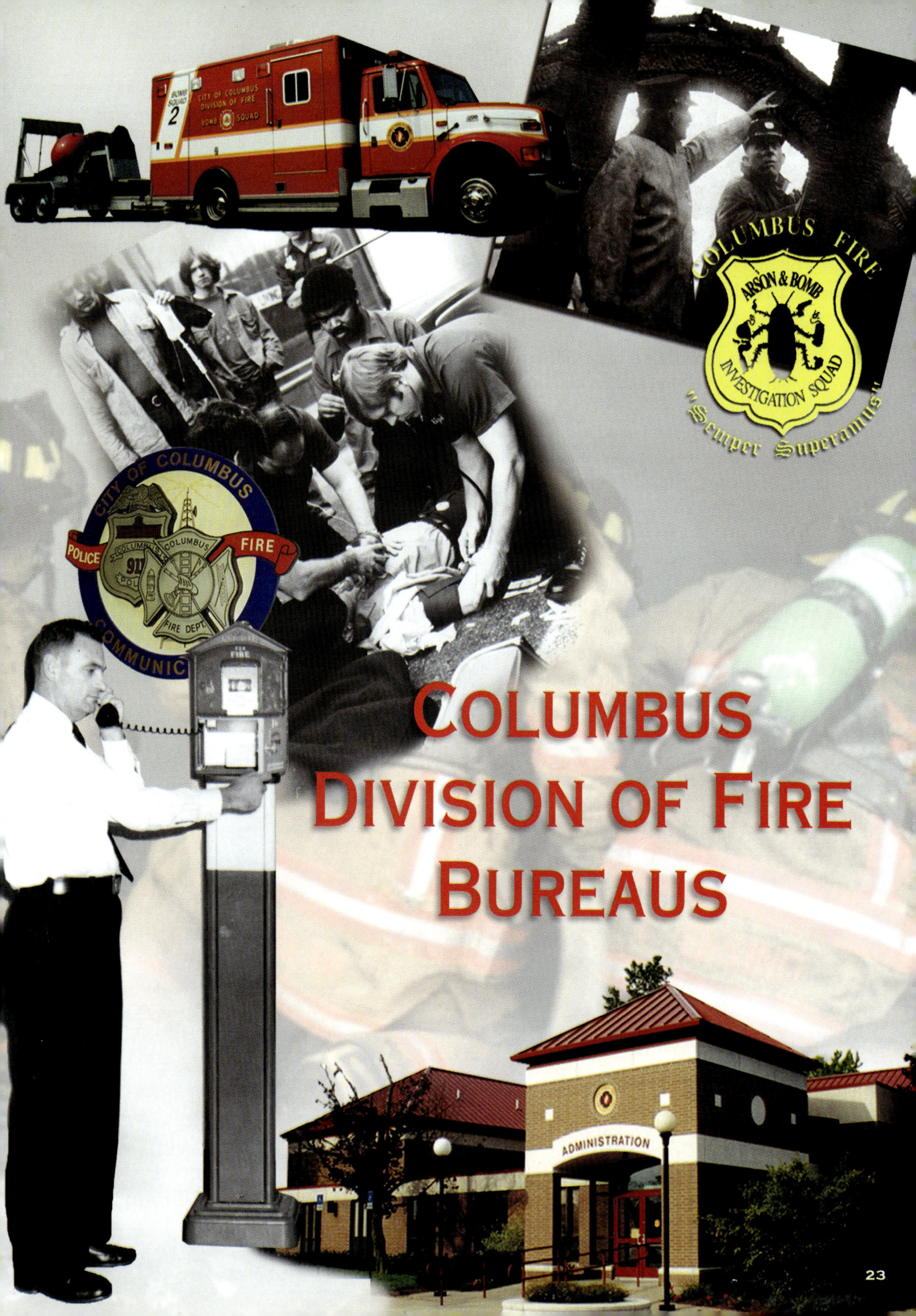

Administration Bureau

The Administrative Manager heads the Administration Bureau. The bureau is separated into two basic areas: Financial Management and Personnel. In these areas, the Bureau provides a wide variety of support and record keeping services for the Division of Fire.

These activities include:
- Submitting, monitoring, and controlling the annual General Fund and Capital Improvement Budget.
- Maintaining a system of accounts receivable and accounts payable, and providing management information reports as needed.
- Administering the payroll, personnel benefits, and the Worker's Compensation reporting system.
- Initiating and monitoring legislation for the Division, as well as monitoring the contractual agreements entered into by the division.
- Assisting the various Bureaus with their computer and information requirements.

Office Of The Chief

The Fire Chief is responsible for ensuring that the Division's resources are utilized efficiently and effectively, thus providing the best possible fire safety and related services to the citizens of Columbus.

Executive Officer

The Executive Officer, Assistant Chief, assists the Fire Chief with the management of the Division by providing administrative oversight and support. All of the Bureaus are organizationally under the direction of the Executive Officer. Two other offices, the Professional Standards Unit and the office of Research and Development, receive direct oversight from the Executive Officer.

The Executive Officer is the Division's disciplinarian, and represents the Division in grievance hearings. He is also the administrator of the Division's Recruitment and Recruit Background Investigations units.

Emergency Services Bureau

The Bureau of Emergency Services is what most people consider to be "The Fire Department." This Bureau is divided into three units, each working a 24 hour shift. Each unit is commanded by a Deputy Chief, who also works a 24 hour shift. The office staff is made up of the Assistant Chief, two firefighters and an Administrative Secretary.

The City is geographically divided into seven Battalions each of which is directed by a Battalion Chief who is responsible for the administration and direction of all activities within their Battalion. Among these seven Battalions there are thirty engine companies, thirty-three engine/medic companies equipped as ALS vehicles, fifteen ladder companies, thirty-one medic transport vehicles, five rescues, hazmat vehicle, bomb unit, eight rescue boats, and seven EMS supervisors.

Emergency Services personnel are involved in many aspects of the Division outside of suppression activities, these include:

- Emergency Medical Services
- Conducting Fire Prevention inspections under the coordination of the Bureau of Fire Prevention
- Instructing recruit firefighters under the direction of the Bureau of Training
- Presenting Fire Safety education programs and fire extinguisher demonstrations under the coordination of the Office of Community Relations
- Juvenile Fire Setters Education
- Fire Safe House programs
- Teaching CPR to High School Students
- Bomb Disposal Unit
- Hazardous Materials Response Team

Emergency Services personnel conduct the majority of Fire Prevention Inspections for the Division, including the quarterly High Rise Inspections conducted by company officers.

Over 23,700 city fire hydrants are flushed clear each spring, pumped dry each fall and inspected regularly by Emergency Services personnel. These inspections help detect hydrants which needed to be repaired or replaced by the Water Shop.

Bomb Disposal Unit

The Columbus Division of Fire Bomb Disposal Unit is one of the largest public safety bomb disposal units in the United States. All 14 technicians are cross trained as Hazardous Material and Weapons of Mass Destruction Technicians and have completed the Hazardous Devices School located in Huntsville, Alabama. After the tragic attacks on the United States on September 11, 2001 the division responded to nearly 700 bio-terrorism incidents.

Hazardous Materials Response Team

The Hazardous Materials Response Team runs out of Fire Station 4 on Winchester Pike. Located in southeast Columbus, it has easy access to the freeway for city-wide response. Prior to 1989, the firefighters on the four heavy rescues responded to haz-mat situations with level "A" suits. In 1989, a dedicated haz-mat team was developed at Station 4 with Engine 4, along with Rescue 15 changing to Rescue 4. Franklin County Commissioners purchased a haz-mat vehicle and all CFD personnel were trained up to awareness level and response level.

Since that time, firefighters at Station 4 and other firefighters throughout the department have increased their training level up to Haz-Mat Technician. Only the members with technician level and the haz-mat physical are allowed to dress in a haz-mat suit at an incident.

The CFD has over 130 members at technician level who may be available to respond on an incident. The Haz-Mat Station responds to approximately 30 haz-mat runs a year. Two major incidents involving CFD were the Orsynex Explosion on September 7, 1989 and the Georgia-Pacific Explosion on September 10, 1997.

Fire Prevention Bureau

The Fire Prevention Bureau is headed by an Assistant Chief and the daily operations are overseen by an Battalion Chief.

The Fire Prevention Bureau's basic responsibilities include:

- Enforcement of the Fire Prevention Codes.
- Reviewing plat plans and building plans for new construction and performing acceptance inspections for new fire protection equipment.
- Providing for the investigation of suspicious, large loss, and incendiary fires and all fire deaths.
- Maintaining all NFIRS reports, fire inspection reports, and fire investigation reports for the Division.

Fire Investigations and Records

The Fire Investigations Section, commonly referred to as Arson Investigations, conduct investigations into the cause of various fires including those of a suspicious, incendiary, or undetermined nature, and all fires involving loss of life or large dollar losses. They also provide follow-up to investigations initiated by Company Officers. The Columbus Fire Arson Investigators are weapon-carrying law enforcement officers, with complete arrest powers.

As a side note: "Woody," the Division's accelerant detection canine, currently works in this section with Firefighter handler Ken Beavers. Woody replaced "Shadow" who retired in 1997. Shadow, along with handler Lt. Bill Bishop, worked 198 fire scenes in 1997 and detected accelerants at 87. Lt. Bishop and Shadow trained at 370 fire scenes, and conducted 28 public demonstrations. As a result of their work, several fire departments from around the country have come to Columbus seeking help to establish their own canine programs.

Inspections Section

The Inspections Section is responsible for providing an effective fire prevention inspection program and enforcing the Fire Prevention Code. The section also reviews plans for new buildings and performs acceptance inspections for new fire protection equipment. Inspections of places of public assembly, night clubs, arcades, and nuisance abatement are also handled by this section.

The Inspections section also converts all City Fire Code numbers to correspond with the Ohio Fire Code, and maintains a current update of all fire codes for the Fire Prevention Bureau reference library.

High Rise Inspection Program

In the High Rise program, each high rise building is assigned to an individual fire company officer who conducts inspections four times a year. This assures that each high rise conforms to current fire codes and fire equipment is properly maintained in the high rise.

Records and Permits Section

This section, under the direction of a Lieutenant, is charged with recording and tabulating statistical data from fire reports submitted by Emergency Services personnel and recording information from the various inspection activities. This section is also responsible for maintaining 17,873 inspection cards and issuing permits.

Plans Review Officer

Plans review is headed up by a Lieutenant who serves as liaison with the Building Department. All plans for new structures are examined for fire safety features.

School Coordinator Officer

The School Coordinator is a Lieutenant who maintains statistical files on primary and secondary schools. This officer has specialized inspection duties and is liaison to these schools relative to problems of a fire protection or fire prevention nature.

Daycare Coordinator Officer

The Daycare Coordinator is also a Lieutenant. This officer coordinates the inspection of nursing homes, hospitals, and group homes as well as daycare centers. By their nature, these types of occupancies present unique life safety problems.

Hazardous Material Coordinator

The Hazardous Materials Coordinator is responsible for insuring that hazardous materials are properly handled and stored. Underground tank and industrial inspections are other duties of this section.

Hydrant Coordinator

The Hydrant Coordinator also works in the Fire Prevention Bureau. The Hydrant Coordinator is responsible for 23,700 city hydrants and 4,592 private hydrants. The hydrant coordinator also is responsible for street plans and associated proposed water mains, both public and private.

Safety Education

Safety Education personnel are involved in many aspects of Community Relations with the motto of "Saving Lives Through Education."

These activities include:
- Evacuation and Escape Planning
- Fire Extinguisher Operation
- Fire Safety Education For Young Children
- Fire Safety Education For Older Children
- Fire Safety Education For Adults

- Fire Safety Education For Retirees
- Fire Safety House
- Fire Safety In The Workplace
- High Rise Evacuation
- Kitchen Safety
- Safe Babysitting
- Smoke Detector Installation and Placement
- Explorer Post #310
- Fire Fighters Against Drugs (FFAD)

Explorer Post #310 was established in 1968. It has been helping young people explore the career of firefighting and emergency medical care for more than 30 years. The Post meets regularly at the Morse Road and Karl Road. Fire Station #24. During these meetings, the scouts practice their first aid skills, and plan participation in upcoming events where they will be able to utilize those skills. Scouts age 18 and older are permitted to ride and observe on emergency runs providing they have met Division and Post requirements.

The Post members assist the Division of Fire in youth programs and fire safety programs. They participate in Post training at the Divisions training facility each summer where they experience many different aspects of Division operations.

FFAD is a youth program sponsored by the Division, which promotes a healthy drug-free lifestyle. The program features several different teaching aspects which build self-esteem, promote responsibility, and educate. TRAPP - Teaches Responsibility, Accountability, Progress, and Potential. Head to Toe teaches personal hygiene and proper diet.

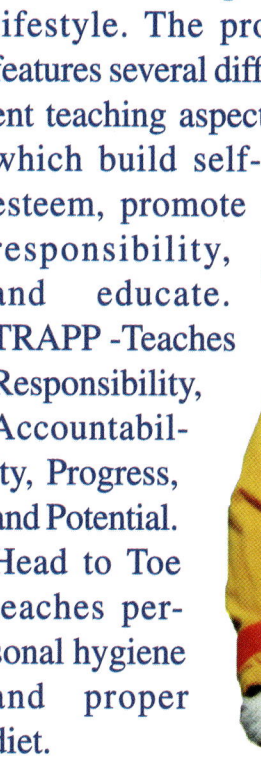

31

Support Services Bureau

The Support Services Bureau was created in 1996's reorganization. This Bureau includes the Fire Alarm Office and the Maintenance Shop. The Support Services Bureau also acts as the Division's liaison with the City of Columbus' Facilities Management and Fleet Management Divisions.

Gamewell Company Fire House Gong
Right : A typical Columbus Gamewell Fire House gong that hung in the apparatus area of the fire house in the early 1900s. As an alarm box was pulled on the street, that box number rang out in the fire houses on the house gong. Firefighters knew where to respond by listening to the number of gong strikes.

Gamewell Company Fire Alarm Street Box
Right middle: A typical fire alarm street box made by the Gamewell Fire Alarm Telegraph Company around 1916. A Columbus street box is identified by its white or silver top and front keyguard painted by the city to make it more visible on the street. The alarm box was activated on the street by citizens to report a fire. The box number was transmitted by telegraph wires to the Fire Alarm Office, where it was received and retransmitted to the fire houses by use of the fire alarm gong system.

Automatic Electric Company Telephone Alarm Box
Right bottom: These boxes were located on Columbus city streets and freeways. These boxes were installed in the early 1960s when the old Gamewell System was removed. The "T" boxes sent alarms from the street to the Fire Alarm Office by voice communication.

33

Training Bureau

The Training Bureau is divided into three offices with a staff of one Battalion Chief, three Captains, one Lieutenant, three Firefighters, and two non-uniformed secretaries. The Mission of the Training Bureau is to assure that all members of the Division of Fire possess the necessary skills and abilities to safety and effectively deal with any situation they might encounter. This responsibility begins the day new firefighters are hired and continues throughout their careers.

Recruit Training

The Recruit Training section is headed by a Captain and his staff of four permanently assigned firefighters. During the 30 week recruit training period, two Lieutenants and several additional firefighter are transferred to this section to assist in supervising and training the recruit firefighters. The Training Bureau graduated two recruit classes, totalling 96 new firefighters in 2000.

Apprenticeship Training

The Apprenticeship Training section is headed by a Captain and has a permanent staff of one Lieutenant and two firefighters. The Apprenticeship Training section is responsible for all aspects of the Apprenticeship Program,

36

including test development, test administration and all associated record keeping. In the year 2001 this section certified 148 firefighters to receive a "Certificate of Completion of Apprenticeship"

EMERGENCY MEDICAL TRAINING

The Emergency Medical Training section is headed by a Captain and his staff of five permanently assigned firefighters, four non-uniformed personnel, and one temporarily assigned Lieutenant who manages the continuing medical education for paramedic personnel. This section provides medical training for all Division members leading to State of Ohio certification as Emergency Medical Technician on either a Basic or Paramedic level. They are also responsible for conducting refresher courses.

OFFICER AND SPECIALIZED TRAINING

A Captain supervises this section including Officer Training, Manual Revision, and Specialized training. He is assisted by one temporarily assigned Lieutenant who oversees the Rescue Technicians Program and one permanently assigned firefighter. Many temporarily assigned uniform personnel or outside facilitators are utilized by this section to offer a wide variety of courses. This section provides ongoing training that keeps our personnel informed of the most current emergency response techniques, and enables them to respond safely and knowledgeably to any emergency.

Recruit Class of 10-31-99

(l. to r.) **Row #1**: Chief Richard Braun, Instructor, Don Brunton, Todd O. Myers, Joshua L. Planck, Ned J. Pettus, David L.McKee, Kevin S. Kruse, Andrew M. Sharpe, Michael D. Woltz, Jason J. Weber, Laura M. Huff, Jill K. Dixon, Michael D. Hays, Gerald C. Butler, Chad M. Girod, Daniel W. Gatley, Richard J. Bakle, and Captain James Cannell. **Row #2**: Instructor Mitch Brooks, Instructor S.W. Bennison, Sean P. Malone, Christopher M. Kennedy, Micah P. Meister, Jon Paul Letki, Timothy C. Maurice, Derrick A. Young, Scott J. Sollars, Joseph A. Simpson, Mark D. Savage, Daniel P. Thompson, Paul N. Given, Robert D. Thompson, Charles Fritz, Jonathan D. Pitzer, Brian J. Heidelman, and Lieutenant George Fulcher. **Row #3**: Instructor David Bernzweig, Kent C. Miller, Michael F. Miles, Richard W. Johnson, Bart A. Molli, Jeffery N. Harris, Rick A. Wagner, Casey C. Vincent, Allen A. Schilling, Darrin D. White, Michael A. Ream, Glenn A. Cecil, Patrick E. Harris, Douglas R. Brown, Todd Bash, Dean C. Gregoroff, and Instructor Steven Herold. **Row #4**: Sean L. Kiess, William W. Loper, Micheal Thompson, Loren D. Peck, Kenneth Montoney, Kavin T. Sturgill, Joel A. Reese, Jed M. Smith, David E. Ulery, Jeffery J. Ross, Dennis J. Hammond, Jeffery T. Ferguson, Thomas A. Sauer, Stephen J. Moehrman, and Lieutenant Michael McKeen. **Row #5**: Scott E. Moore, Jeff A. Lyon, Kurt E. Jezek, James O. Zwayer, Matthew J. Robertson, Thomas J. Scholl, Mark E. Wiley, Michael J. Thornhill, Dennis J. Sheridan, Anthony V. Ulery, Mike A. Gischel, Byron J. Garnes, Harold J. Chambers, and Lieutenant David Hennosy.

Recruit Class of 7-23-00

(l. to r.) **Back row**: Instructor Henry Sexton, Act. Lt. Larry Harrow, Instructor Steve Herold, Michael Reed, Stephen Peer, Melvin Hart, Joseph Shoaf, Deric Scott, Matt Woessner, Gregory Woods, and Troy Knode. **Middle row**: Scott Kulpa, Jeffrey Stanforth, Michael Windon, Greg Weber, Michael Lesko, Thomas Eckenrode, Jared Saling, Jeff Mitchell, Asst. Chief Richard Braun, Capt. James Lewis, and Lt. George Fulcher. **Front row**: Chad Bates, Kenneth Rookard, Aaron Hageman, Thad Turano, Michael Pontones, John Cash, Jason Davis, and Stuart Madison.

Recruit Class of 5-14-00

1. FF Roger Andersen, Act. Capt. James Cannell, FF Ken Peters, Ricky Ratcliff, Randy Kauffeld, Brian Wilson, Leland Dye, Steve Carna, Sean McCray, Cory Crudet, Anthony Tinnerman, FF Mitch Brooks, Act. Lt. Larry Harrow, and Lt. Michael McKeen. 2. Act. Lt. George Fulcher, Holly Hanf, Laura Lang, William Nelson, Melissa Mohler, Dwayne Crum, Mike Seed, FF Steve Herold, Act. Lt. George Roback, and Bn. Chief Robert Babb. 3. Donald Gaber, Tim Brintlinger, Kevin Tackett, Jesse Williams, William Hall, Shawn Farley, Jim Gray, Mike Palermo, Brian Snyder, and Rodney Dommer.

Supplementary Groups of the CDF

Columbus Ohio Division of Fire Auxiliary

The Columbus Ohio Auxiliary Fire Department started during the war years of 1942 through 1946, to assist the Columbus Fire Department keep its fire companies up to manpower standards and to make up for the members who were called up for the war effort. By City Charter the Auxiliary became a part of the Civil Defense effort. In 1970, the Columbus Auxiliary Fire Department name was changed to the Columbus Ohio Division of Fire Auxiliary.

Box 15

In 1947, fifteen Columbus men, led by a pharmacist named Max Haverman, joined together to give direction and purpose to their firefighting interests. "Doc" Haverman knew most of Columbus' firemen and they knew him. As the first president of the new club, the Box 15 Club, Max worked hard at having the group make a positive lasting impression on the Columbus Fire Department. Incidentally, "Box 15," when Columbus had the Gamewell System of fire alarm boxes mounted on telephone poles, was located at Long and Lexington. Max noted it had no great significance. The "15" referred to the number of members in the club.

Box 15 in 2001

For many years, the club held rigidly to its rule of fifteen active members and fifteen associate members. You could become an active member only if a current active member retired or died and your name was at the top of the associate list. The active membership quota was eventually expanded to thirty.

As the club developed its activities through the 1950s & 1960s the canteen service it performed became paramount. Members carried insulated jugs in the trunks of their cars along with a supply of instant coffee, cocoa, lemonade, and cups. After learning of a fire either by monitor radio or a "call list" of members, Box 15 personnel would report to the fire scene. With the permission of the officer in charge, they would begin distributing refreshments to weary firefighters.

In 1974 Box 15 purchased an old squad vehicle from the Columbus Fire Department. In 1980, Box 15 entered into agreements with the Salvation Army to use the "Sallies" modern, well-equipped mobile canteens. In 1986 the Volunteer Firemen's Resource Organization gave the club grant money to purchase a nearly new van to replace the red van. In August of 1996, a decommissioned 1985 EMS vehicle was purchased with money raised through the sale of t-shirts and sweatshirts by Box 15 members. It resides at Station 30 and is used as Box 15's secondary unit. Box 15's primary unit, residing at Station 1, is a 1991 Horton, acquired in early 2000.

Box 15's primary role in the fire service is that of rehabilitation, a.k.a. rehab. Rehab, in the fire service, provides essential liquids for re-hydration of exhausted firefighters, as well as cooling them down. Box 15 responds automatically to most greater alarm fires within the City of Columbus, as well as most other fire departments in Central Ohio.

In 2001, Box 15 responded to 33 incidents and provided beverage (and in some instances food) services for approximately 2000 personnel.

4-Unit

The first recorded meeting of the Columbus Fire Retirees Club (4-Unit) was on June 7, 1978. Ray Beougher was Acting Chairman. The primary reason for this meeting was to get the club organized and nominations were held for the election of officers.

At the July 7, 1978 meeting the first officers of the organization were elected. They were President Eddie Manns, Secy/Treas Tom Sides, and Sgt. At Arms Don Braskett.

Firemens Park, Buckeye Lake

In November 1979 the club voted to become affiliated with the Police and Fire Retirees of Ohio, an affiliation still in effect today.

In August of 1981 the club voted to admit all paid Firefighter Retirees of Central Ohio to the organization. In October of 1982 the club changed their name to the Central Ohio Retired Firefighters.

In May of 1985 the first trustees of the organization were elected. They were Jim Wolfe, Bert Green and Don Fadley.

In 1986 two members of the organization were elected to offices of the Police and Fire Retirees of Ohio. Tom McDonald was elected president and Henry Reeb was elected trustee.

The first 4-Unit News was published in December 1986. The newspaper is currently published bimonthly and is edited by John and Judy Cahill, the editors since inception.

Today Central Ohio Retired Firefighters (4-Unit) is a thriving, growing fraternal organization with 550+ members. They have monthly meetings to conduct business and socialize, a bi-monthly newsletter, a bi-annual roster, annual picnic and golf league. On the more serious side, the organization, along with its affiliate the Police and Fire Retirees of Ohio, sponsors and lobbys for legislation that positively affects all fire and police retirees in Ohio.

4 Unit at 2001 Meeting

The Central Ohio Fire Museum

Through the combined efforts of Central Ohio firefighters, community and corporate leaders, over $684,000 was raised to complete the authentic restoration of the exterior of No. 16 Engine House, located at 260 N. Fourth Street.

The next phase of the project is to renovate the first floor interior, design and build displays, and develop "hands-on" life saving exhibits programmed for school children.

For generations, firefighters have risked their lives to help their communities in the time of need. Some have paid the ultimate price by dying in the line of duty.

The Central Ohio Fire Museum & Learning Center will pay tribute to our firefighters, past, present and future, and the rich legacy they have left us. Through a collection of hand-drawn, horse-drawn and motorized fire apparatus, visitors will be able to retrace the steps of firefighters and learn about their day-to-day lives in the engine house.

The Learning Center will reach over 30,000 children annually with educational and interactive displays. Fire prevention education programming and life saving procedures for the entire family will be offered on a year round basis.

"Learning from the past to save lives in the future"

54 Wonders

As the City of Columbus and the Division of Fire exited the severe and lengthy Depression in January of 1941, the Fire Department offered many benefits not provided in the private sector: "25 year pension, vacation with pay, 24 hours on and 24 hours off duty with a 7th day off named, a Kelly Day along with $150.00 pay each month."

This made many look closely at the Fire Department. Then proceeding to take the tests, physical exam first, passing and moving on to the written test. An eligibility list was established and there were 54 new firefighters selected.

Fire Chief Welch organized the 1st Fire Training program; conducted at "Drill School", using several instructors, covering hose evolution, pump operations, ladder use, ropes, tools, driving, tilling, and simplified hydraulics. Captain Zwayer was quoted as saying "These 54 men, after completing drill school, will come to company with more skills than a 3 year fireman." Upon hearing this someone retorted, "I can't wait to meet one of these 54 Wonders." Thus the 54 Wonders began their career.

In 1941, 17 of the 19 engine houses were built for horse drawn apparatus, the horses and the storage of hay. They were heated by coal fired, "pot belly" stoves. Wool blankets better suited for the horses and cane Delaware chairs were produced by the Ohio Penitentiary inmates for the engine houses.

World War II took 19 of the 54 to serve our country in every branch of service. One would not return, a bombardier by the name of Paul D. Robinson. He was killed in a bomber crash returning to England in 1944.

Now the "53 Wonders" in 1946 were back home and on the job. Things had changed, including apparatus. They proceeded to work diligently at bettering themselves and the Division of Fire.

Their contributions to the Columbus Division of Fire include: Implementing the 3 Platoon system we have today (the 56 hour work week), Since reduced to 48 hours, the Columbus Fire Drill manual, Local 67 News, cartoons, fuel and tank inspections, baby sitter training, The Benevolent Fund, minstrel shows, water safety instruction given by the Fire Department at Ohio State University to the students, purchase and movement of the Credit Union to its current location. Firefighter march for muscular dystrophy, IAFF local 67 as the sole bargaining power, heroic acts of the 1959 flood, purchase and management of the Buckeye Lake Fireman's Park, teaching first aid classes, Local 67's Industrial Compensation Representative, Firefighters Memorial, Charity Newsies, and Faithful service to all the Military branches during WWII.

Although these men did not organize the Columbus Division of Fire, they were instrumental with the assistance of all to mold our department into what it is today.

First Row: 1. Paul Fribley 2. Robert Moore 3. Frank Grashel 4. Herb Barrett 5. Sam Zaayer 6. Glen Barr 7. George Brown 8. Russ Witt 9. Val Boehm 10. Ed Manns 11. Pete Angelo **Second Row:** 15. Paul Hearn 16. Ray Hartsock 17. Dick Reidling 18. Bob Gerstner 19. Bill Solomon 20. Dan Bonzo 2. Loui Cennano 22. George Mick **Third Row:** 12. Ray Devine 13. Bob Moss 14. Ed Kamer 23. Ed Hart 24. Paul Robinson 25. Francis Every 26. Leo Houck 27. Art Whitaker 28. Pat O'Brien **Fourth Row:** 29. Chas. Highland 30. Dick Diebel 31. Ray Hysell 32. Chas. Stewart 33. Joe Moody 34. Tom Staley 35. Charles Smith 36. Leroy Bowman 37. Bill Dulin **Fifth Row:** 38. Ted Schneider 39. Paul Davis 40. Ray Beougher 41. Chas. Craig 42. Trenten Howells 43. Frank Phipps 44. Art Grimm 45. Ralph Neff 46. E.G. Landen 47. Bob Brannon **Sixth Row:** 48. Dick Evans 49. Paul Buchannon 50. Kenny Gilbert 51. Jim Seagle 52. Kenny Musser 53. Bob Welch 54. Dave Sting 55. Bob Crane 56. Bill Seitz 57. Vinney Myers. Paul Robinson was killed in WW II. Captain Zaayer was in charge assisted by Captain Brown and G. Barr. Picture taken by P. Angelo

CISM Team

Team leader Assistant Chief Dan Vincent, FPB
Mental Health Advisor Kay Werk, Netcare
Coordinator Assistant Chief Carl Lawhorn, Executive Office
Peer Support Leader Firefighter Vic Runkle, R-2, 3 unit

Peer Support Members
One Unit
Bn. Chief Chief Butcher, U/A, Bn. 5
Bn. Chief Flynn, Bn. 3*
Bn. Chief Paxton, Bn. 5
Lt. Jim Davis, R/O, Bn. 1
Lt. Russ Barton, EMS 16
Lt. Tom DeLong, EMS 13
Lt. Larry Hilbert, E-23
Lt. Rodney Smith, L-15
Lt. Mike Zuber, E-13
FF Tom Bruno, E-18
FF Mark Evans, E-21
FF Gary Greiner, E-19
FF Steve Heughebart, E-18
FF Dave Karn, R-2*
FF Tim Kynion, E-2
FF Kari Linberg, E-14
FF John Moore, TR-25
FF Ed Ongaro, E-11
FF Rich Thompson, Jr., E-17
FF Tannis Vaughn, EMS 22
FF Tom Wake, R-2
FF Bill Williams, R-17

Two Unit
Bn. Chief Rick Gaal, Bn. 4
Bn. Chief Craig Mosley, R/O, Bn. 7
Capt. Terry Cordle, EMS 11*
Capt. Greg Lash, L-1*
Capt. Dave Whiting, L-15
Capt. Rick Boham, R/O, Bn. 1
Lt. Robert Cloud, E-2
Lt. Jeff Happ, R/O, Bn. 5
Lt. John Hill, L-13
Lt. Mike Vedra, ES-1
FF Mike Adams, E-28
FF John Barrett, E-2
FF Doug Behrens, L-1
FF David Blair, R-16
FF Barb Capuana, E-30
FF Dave Hall, E-33
FF Scott Hammock, E-2*
FF Stuart Mack, L-1
FF Eric Norman, E-15
FF Tommie Page, E-28
FF Price Smith, L-15
FF Dave Wittman, R-2

Three Unit
Dep. Chief Ned Pettus, ES-2
Bn. Chief Mason, Bn. 5
Bn. Chief Doug Smith, Bn.4
Bn. Chief Wintering, Bn. 7
Capt. John Vingle, L-13
Lt. Garey Borgan, E-23
Lt. Carl Stone, L-26
Lt. Monte Williamson, E-20
FF John Brining, R-2*
FF John Cheatham, E-23
FF Kelly Green, R-11
FF Mark Humphrey, L-10
FF Mark Holt, TR-25
FF Tom Hughes, R-2
FF Wallace Jackson, R-4
FF Ron Lautzenheiser, E-4
FF Vic Runkle, R-2*
FF Mark Siemer, R-2
FF Jeff Stanley, E-3
FF Sam Trapasso, E-14
FF Steve Treinish, L-2
FF Rodney Warner, E-2
FF Mark Werner, E-2

*Denotes Peer Support Contacts For Each Unit

40 Hours
Msgr. Colby Grimes
Mary Humphrey, RN, O.S.U.
Toni Rausch, EMS
Capt. Jerry Goss, Exec. Off.
Capt. Wes Fullen, FPB
Lt. Bernie Nance, TA
FF George Fulcher, TA
FF Josh Brent, FPB
FF Duane Landis, Background
FF Tom Morton, Bn. 1
FF Monte Robinson, Arson
FF Larry Patrick, Ret.
FF Robert Steele, Ret.

Netcare mental Health
Karen Beardman, Netcare
Lisa Callander, EAP
Kappy Madenwald
Scott Johnson, Comp. Drug
Karen Roberts
Cathy Hill, Nationwide
Sharon Saia, Netcare
Kay Perkins, Netcare

Township Members
D/Chief Keith Larsen, Jackson Twp.
Capt. Gary Jones, Madison Twp., 2 Unit
Capt. Gary Rugh, Jackson Twp.
FF Bob Bishop, Washington Twp., 1 Unit
FF Mike Cooper, Upper Arlington, 2 Unit
FF John Hill, Violet Twp., 1 Unit
FF Jim King, Washington Twp., 3 Unit
FF Jim Starrett, Upper Arlington, 3 Unit
FF David Bruns, Westerville, 1 Unit
FF Tom Ullon, Westerville, 1 Unit
FF Jim Paxton, Violet Twp., 3 Unit
FF Mike Litteral, Worthington, 3 Unit
FF Paul Grutsch, Franklin Twp., 1 Unit
FF Lou Hoyer, Upper Arlington, 2 Unit
FF Dan Swords, Jackson Twp., 2 Unit
FF Steven Veselica, Jackson Twp.
FF Robert Zvansky, Worthington, 3 Unit

Assistant Chief Daniel Vincent
Health Advisor, Kay Werk
Ret. Assistant Chief Richard Cline

What are they Now?

Engine House No. 5
Restaurant

Engine House No. 6
Jimmy Rea Electronics

Engine House No. 7
"The Rock" – Offices

Engine House No. 12
Music Hall

Engine House No. 17
Hilltop Community Center

The oldest active Firehouse in Columbus is station #10 located at 1096 W. Broad St. Construction began in August 1896 and was completed in February 1897. The total cost of the engine house, horses, harness, hose and apparatus was $22,139.69. Over one hundred years later, Engine house #10 still serves the citizens of Columbus.

Although, Station 10 is the oldest active firehouse, there are a few older ones still standing. Engine houses 7 & 8 were both built in 1888. Station #8 is located on North 20th, near Mt. Vernon Ave. and station #7 at Euclid St. & Pearl Al. The original Station 5 on Thurman Ave. is now a popular restaurant and old Station 6 at Mill & W. Broad St. is now an electronics store, both were built in 1892.

Other non-active houses are #11 1000 E. Main St.(1897), #12 Oak St. & Marble Al. (1892), #14 Parson's Ave. & Hinman (1906), and #17 2300 W. Broad St. (1897). Most notable of all the old firehouses is #16 at 260 N. Fourth St. (1908) which has been restored to it's original beauty on the outside and when restored on the inside will house the Central Ohio Fire Museum.

Active vintage firehouses include: #18 1551 Cleveland Ave. (1926) and #19 3601 N. High St. (1931).

ATHLETICS

45

46

47

48

49

COLUMBUS DIVISION OF FIRE AWARDS

Silver Maltese

Medal of Valor

Bronze Maltese

Distinguished Service Award

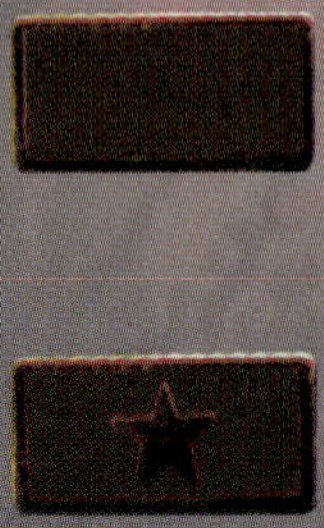

Fire Chiefs Award

Fire Service Award of Merit

Multiple

Multiple

Multiple

Columbus Division of Fire Stations

FIRE DEPARTMENT HEADQUARTERS

The first mention of a specific location for the Chief's office was in the 1872 Annual Report (for 1871). It listed the Chief's office in the Gay Street Engine House. In 1872 the Third Street Engine House was remodeled, enlarged to three bays and the Chief moved in here.

In 1891, the first official Fire Department Headquarters was opened at the southwest corner of Elm and Front Street. It was designated Engine House #1 and was built at a cost of $38,000. Several parcels of land were purchased for the station and one parcel was willed to the department as long as the fire department continued to occupy the property. The station was three stories tall, of a Gothic Design and constructed of brick and stone. The bell tower rose 120 feet above the ground. The station housed fire companies, the headquarters offices and the fire alarm office and equipment.

During the 1930's the engine house began to deteriorate faster than it could be repaired, and in 1939 the Chief and the fire alarm office began moving to new quarters in City Hall. In 1941 the building department began condemnation proceedings, and in 1944 the last fire apparatus moved out. Old Station 1 would remain empty until razed in 1954.

It had been hoped that a new headquarters building would be built on the old Front Street location, but it would be almost 25 years later that a new headquarters complex would be built on Greenlawn Avenue. Located at 200 Greenlawn Avenue next to the Scioto River, the new complex was opened July 27, 1962. The entire complex consisted of the Administrative building, a communications building for Police and Fire radio repair, a fire training tower and training academy, and maintenance and vehicle repair buildings.

In 1995, the department moved into a remodeled high school that would house a new administrative complex and training academy. The new complex is located on the south side of Columbus at 3675 Parsons Avenue. The old headquarters building on Greenlawn Avenue was turned over to other city departments.

The new administrative building houses all fire department administrative functions as well as the Chief's office.

The main high school building houses the following amenities:

- Full size gymnasium for fire department use
- Auditorium for classes and presentations
- Cafeteria and vending area for meals
- EMS offices
- EMS classrooms
- EMS medical supply
- Special duty vehicle garage
- Training Academy classrooms and locker rooms
- Photo Lab
- Fire Prevention Bureau
- Community Relations
- Recruiting and Background Investigations
- Mask Repair
- Tools and Equipment
- Fully equipped exercise room

CFD Battalions

BATTALION 1

STATION 1 — Built 1982
300 North Fourth Street
Engine 1
Ladder 1
Engine 9
Medic 1
ES-2
SO-2
Tow One
EMS-11

STATION 2 — Built 1962
150 East Fulton Street
Engine 2
Ladder 2
Engine 3
Rescue 2
Medic 2
Battalion 1
Bomb Squad
Boat 2

STATION 8 — Built 1968
1240 East Long Street
Engine 8
Ladder 8
Medic 8

STATION 25 — Built 1961
739 West Third Avenue
Engine 25
Medic 25

BATTALION 2

STATION 6 — Built 1969
5750 Maple Canyon Avenue
Engine 6
Medic 6
Battalion 2
Boat 6
EMS-12

STATION 24 — Built 1960
1585 Morse Road
Engine 24
Ladder 24
Medic 24

STATION 28 — Built 1981
3240 McCutcheon
Engine 28
Ladder 28
Medic 28

STATION 29 — Built 1984
5151 Little Turtle Way
Engine 29
Medic 29

STATION 33 — Built 1981
440 Lazelle Road
Engine 33
Ladder 33
Medic 33
EMS 12

BATTALION 3

STATION 7 — Built 1966
1425 Indianola Avenue
Engine 7
Medic 7
Battalion 3
Boat 7
EMS-13

STATION 13 — Built 1957
309 Arcadia Avenue
Engine 13
Ladder 13
Medic 13
Boat 13

STATION 16 — Built 1952
1130 East Weber Road
Engine 16
Rescue 16
Medic 16

STATION 18 Built 1926
1551 Cleveland Avenue
Engine 18
Medic 18

BATTALION 4

STATION 4 — Built 1976
3030 Winchester Pike
Engine 4
Medic 4
Hazmat 4
Rescue 4

STATION 14 — Built 2001
1514 Parsons Avenue
Engine 14
Battalion 4
Medic 14
Boat 14

STATION 15 — Built 1968
1800 East Livingston Avenue
Engine 15
Ladder 15
EMS 14
Medic 15

STATION 22 — Built 1959
3069 Parsons Avenue
Engine 22
Medic 22
Ladder 22
Boat 22

STATION 32 — Built 1991
3675 Gender Road
Engine 32
Ladder 32
Medic 32

BATTALION 5

STATION 10 — Built 1896
1096 West Broad Street
Engine 10
Ladder 10
Medic 10

STATION 12 — Built 1950
3200 Sullivant Avenue
Engine 12
Ladder 12
Medic 12

STATION 17 — Built 1994
2250 West Broad Street
Engine 17
Rescue 17
Medic 17
Battalion 5
EMS 15

STATION 26 — Built 1974
5433 Fisher Road
Engine 26
Medic 26
Ladder 26

STATION 31 — Built 1988
5305 Alkire Road
Engine 31
Medic 31
Tank 31

BATTALION 6

STATION 5 — Built 1972
211 NcNaughten Road
Engine 5
Medic 5
EMS-16

STATION 20 — Built 1950
2646 East Fifth Avenue
Engine 20
Medic 20

STATION 21 — Built 1950
3294 East Main Street
Engine 21
Battalion 6
Medic 21
Boat 21

STATION 23 — Built 1959
4451 East Livingston Avenue
Ladder 23
Engine 23
Medic 23

BATTALION 7

STATION 11 — Built 1991
2200 West Case Road
Aircrash 1
Engine 11
Rescue 11
Battalion 7
Medic 11
EMS 17

STATION 19 — Built 1929
3601 North High Street
Engine 19
Medic 19

STATION 27 — Built 1978
7560 Smokey Row Road
Engine 27
Medic 27
Ladder 27

STATION 30 — Built 1988
3555 Fishinger Blvd
Engine 30
Medic 30
Boat 30

Station One

The Columbus volunteer fire department was organized in 1822 and consisted of volunteer firefighters supplied with some axes, ladders and buckets.

First Engine House

The first building mentioned for fire protection was in 1824. It was a small wood building called Capitol Square Engine House. It housed a hand-drawn, hand pumping "engine" and was located on State property set aside for the future Capitol building.

In 1835, the City was authorized to erect a more permanent engine house, but on the condition that the site had to be vacated when the Statehouse was to be built. It wasn't until 1852 that the City actually built a building on the Statehouse site, again called the Capitol Engine House. The equipment and volunteer crews were called the

ACHIEVEMENT

Engine 1, 1935

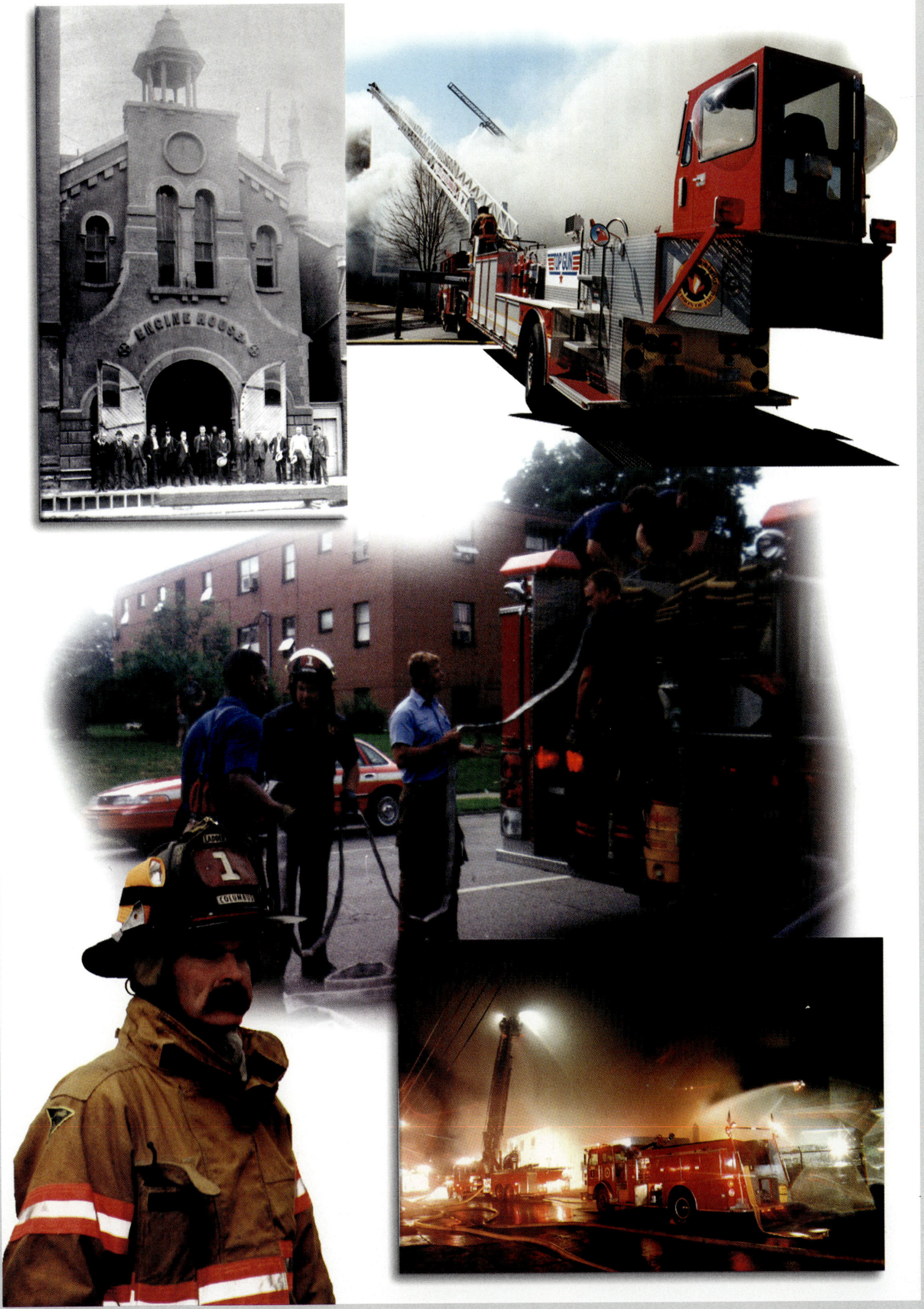

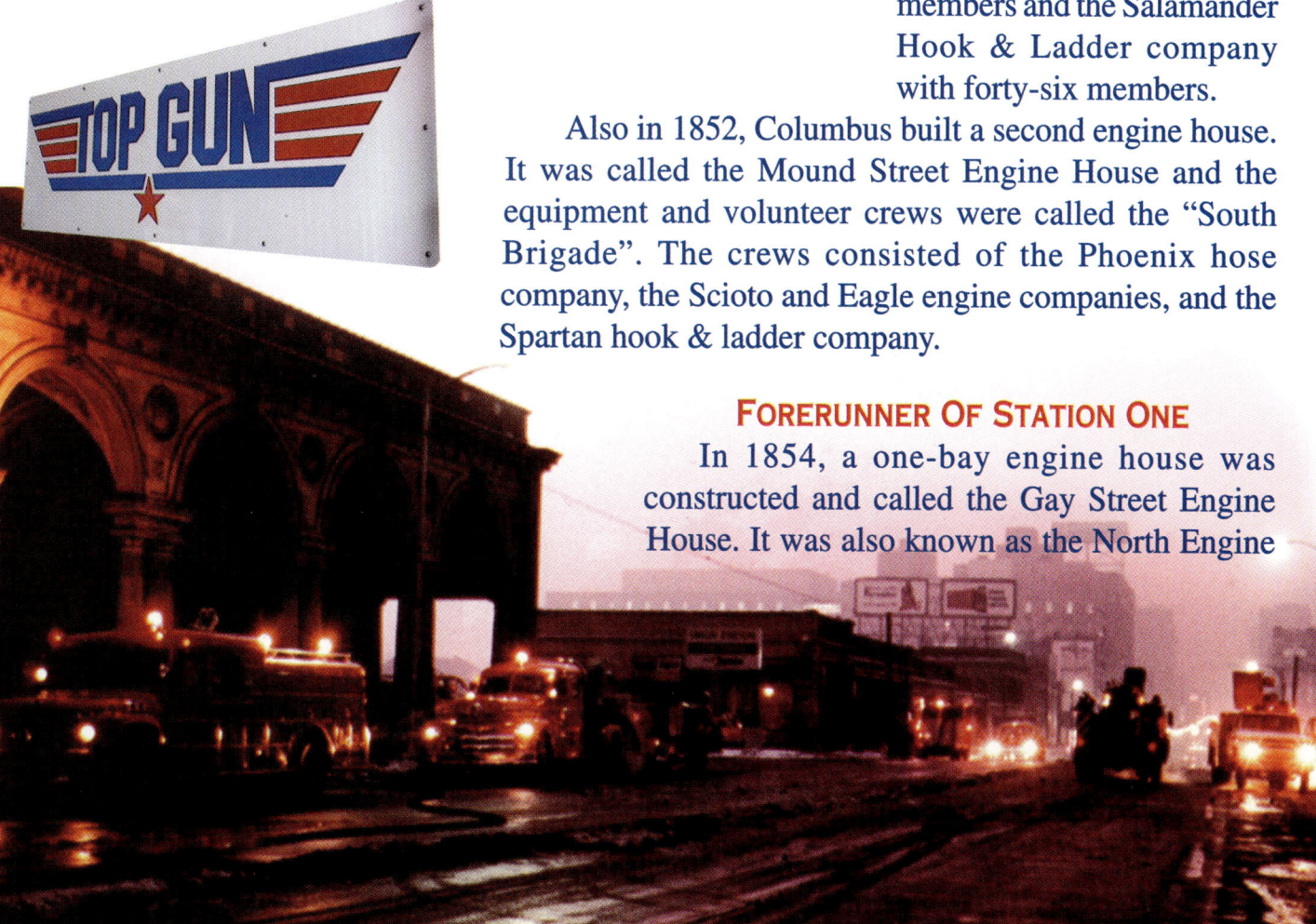

"North Brigade". The crews consisted of the Franklin engine with forty-one members, the Hornet hose company with thirty-six members and the Salamander Hook & Ladder company with forty-six members.

Also in 1852, Columbus built a second engine house. It was called the Mound Street Engine House and the equipment and volunteer crews were called the "South Brigade". The crews consisted of the Phoenix hose company, the Scioto and Eagle engine companies, and the Spartan hook & ladder company.

Forerunner Of Station One

In 1854, a one-bay engine house was constructed and called the Gay Street Engine House. It was also known as the North Engine

House and would later become the first engine house designated "No. 1". It originally housed a hand engine called the "Fame", but it was replaced around 1860 with a new Silsby steamer and a hose reel. It is not known how both fit in the one-bay station. In 1864 this building was the only engine house to have a bell for signaling the location of fires. Bells in churches, schools, the market house or the courthouse gave alarms of fire in the various districts of the city.

In 1891 the first official Fire Department Headquarters was opened at the southwest corner of Elm and Front Street. It was designated Engine House #1 and was built at a cost of $38,000. Several parcels of land were purchased for the station and one parcel was willed to the department as long as the fire department continued to occupy the property. The station was three stories tall, of a Gothic Design and constructed of brick and stone. The bell tower rose 120 feet above the ground. The station housed fire companies, the headquarters offices and the fire alarm office and equipment.

During the 1930's the engine house began to deteriorate faster than it could be repaired, and in 1939 the fire alarm office began moving to new quarters in City Hall. In 1941 the building department began condemnation proceedings, and in 1944 the last fire apparatus moved out. Old Station 1 would remain empty until razed in 1954.

There would not be another Station #1 until 1953 when a new Station 16 was opened at Weber and McGuffey. The old Engine House #16 at Chestnut and Fourth was renamed Station 1 and would occupy this site until 1981 when a new modern three-story concrete station would be built one block north of old 16's.

1982
First Floor-Seven bays front and rear, quarters for EMS personnel, 2 Engines/1 Ladder/1 Medic/ 1 EMS supervisor/1 Assistant Chief, 1 Cave-In/1 Mass Casualty/1 High-Rise. **Second Floor**-FF living quarters, Assistant Chief Office, Fire Prevention Bureau. **Third Floor**-Arson Bureau/Bomb Squad offices and lab, one room utilized for exercise equipment. The remainder is planned for the future alarm office and other expansion.

1983-1984
The Alarm Office moved from the 4th floor of City Hall to the 3rd floor of Station 1. Facilities included a kitchen, restrooms, 8 bedrooms, and the FAO chiefs' office.

57

1993

Alarm office consolidated with Police dispatching in common building (but separate dispatching areas) on Fairwood Avenue. Old alarm office space taken over by Community Relations offices and personnel until new complex completed on Parsons Avenue in 1995.

Professional Standards Unit (Internal Affairs) occupies new space on third floor, along with Background Investigations (recruiting). The Division Historian also established an office on the third floor.

1995

Background Investigations' third floor offices move to Parsons Avenue. Historian expands into their office space. Community Relations also moves to Parsons and Arson Bureau takes over their space.

The Fire Prevention Bureau also moves to Parsons Avenue from its second floor offices.

2000

Professional Standards Unit moves from third floor to newly renovated space in old FPB space. Also created are new offices for safety officer and rescue training officer.

Station Two

Fourth Engine House Built (forerunner of Station 2)

In 1859, a new engine house called the South Street Engine House was constructed at the southeast corner of South High Street and South Street (now called Fulton Street). The station faced High Street and cost $2,247 to build. It was a two-bay, two-story station.

A hand engine operated from here with volunteers until July 1863 when a new Silsby Steamer was purchased. It cost $4,000 and was named the "John Miller" in honor of the first Chief Engineer (Fire Chief). The horse stall doors were connected by a trip wire to the station gong. When the gong sounded the doors opened, allowing the horses to take their places at the apparatus unassisted. At this time the volunteer crew became full-time paid members of the department.

By 1875, the engine house had fallen into an unsafe condition. On October 2, 1876 city council passed a resolution instructing the fire committee to proceed with bids to rebuild the engine house. On February 6, 1877-just 97 days later-the house

Engine 2 crew, 1913

BRAVERY

was completed at a cost of $4,394. Members of the department did the tearing down of the old engine house and cleaning of the old brick. In 1883 a new two-tank chemical engine replaced the 1863 steamer. The new engine had 300 feet of one-inch rubber hose and was purchased at a cost of $2,300. In 1890, the department returned to the use of steamers, however the engine house was too small and the wood floor too weak to safely house a steamer.

In 1892, the South Street Engine House was one of five engine houses rebuilt to accommodate the re-introduction of steamers to the department. It was rebuilt as a two-story, three-bay station at the southeast corner of Fulton and Pearl. It was re-named the Fulton Street Engine House and cost $23,590. A new No. 1 Size Ahrens 1000 gallon per minute steamer was purchased which replaced the chemical engine. In 1894 an aerial ladder made by the Fire Extinguisher Manufacturing Co. was placed in service. It had an 82-foot aerial ladder and 275 feet of ground ladders and required a two-horse hitch. In 1904, a new aerial that had a smaller capacity replaced it, but was heavier and required a three-horse hitch. In 1918, both the steamer and aerial ladder were motorized with tractors. The station remained in service until 1962 when it was razed to make way for the Interstate Freeway system and the new Market-Mohawk redevelopment project.

In 1962, a new engine house was constructed at Fulton and South Fourth. This was necessitated by the construction of the interstate freeway system and the Market-Mohawk redevelopment project. In December 1962, old engine house 2 and 3 were vacated and combined in the new station named Station #2. The equipment from Engine House 2 was combined with Engine House 3's equipment as a matter of economics, since the original engine houses were only a few blocks apart. Each engine has its own response area, Engine 2 responds south and Engine 3 responds north of the engine house.

Opened in December 1962, Station 2 is a one-story station with apparatus bays in the center and living quarters on the ends. The station cost $296,622. The equipment responds to downtown Columbus and the surrounding freeway system. Station 2 also houses Heavy Rescue #2, one of the busiest rescues in the country. Bomb Squad 2 also is housed here, one of the very few fire department operated Bomb Squads in the nation. Equipment responding from Station #2 includes two engines, an aerial platform, a Battalion Chief, the Rescue, the Bomb Squad and a Medic.

63

President George Bush's Visit

Fulton and S. 4th Streets

Station Three

The Columbus Volunteer Fire Department was organized in 1822 and consisted of volunteer firefighters supplied with some axes, ladders and buckets.

First Engine House 1824

The first building mentioned for fire protection was in 1824. It was a small wood building called Capitol Square Engine House. It housed a hand-drawn, hand pumping "engine" and was located on State property set aside for the future Capitol building.

In 1835, the City was authorized to erect a more permanent engine house, but on the condition that the site had to be vacated when the Statehouse was to be built. It wasn't until 1852 that the City actually

CARING

Engine 3. June 27, 1928

built a building on the Statehouse site, again called the Capitol Engine House. The equipment and volunteer crews were called the "North Brigade". The crews consisted of the Franklin engine with forty-one members, the Hornet hose company with thirty-six members and the Salamander Hook & Ladder Company with forty-six members.

First Engine House No. 3

In 1855, the City was notified to vacate the Statehouse property. A new engine house was built at Third Street and Chapel and was called the Third Street Engine House. This replaced the Capitol Engine House previously located on the Statehouse property. In 1858, Columbus purchased its first steamer that required special care and horses that required full-time care and feeding. This resulted in the first paid crew and the Columbus Fire Department now became a "paid" department. In October 1864, local insurance companies purchased a hook and ladder truck for the department. It was named "Gift" and was housed here with the steamer. In 1872 the National Board of Fire Underwriters purchased a salvage wagon for the use of the department. In 1876, they purchased another salvage wagon to replace the 1872 wagon. It was also a chemical engine with an 80 gallon tank, 200 feet of 3/4 hose, 25 tarps, axes,

THE DONALDSON

Third Street Engine House

and brooms. They also supplied ten "minutemen" to do salvage work at the fire.

In 1872, the engine house was remodeled at a cost of $4,080 and received a new front, new bay floor and a second story. It was renamed the Donaldson Engine House after Luther Donaldson, a prominent member of the fire committee. During the remodeling, the new oak floor was placed directly on the ground with no drainage. After four years of stabling horses on the floor, a sickening odor began to permeate the house. In June 1876 three members were stricken with typhoid fever at one time.

In 1877 the problem was remedied with a new concrete floor. In 1888 the department purchased its first aerial ladder, an 85 foot spring-raised ladder.

In 1894 the station was once again remodeled and renamed, this time to No. 3 Engine House. The engine house was enlarged to three bays and housed a steamer, hose wagon and an 85 foot aerial ladder. In 1902 the aerial was moved to #1 house and was replaced by a Champion water tower. All of the horse-drawn equipment was motorized in 1918, and in 1923, the station received a Seagrave Gorman pumper.

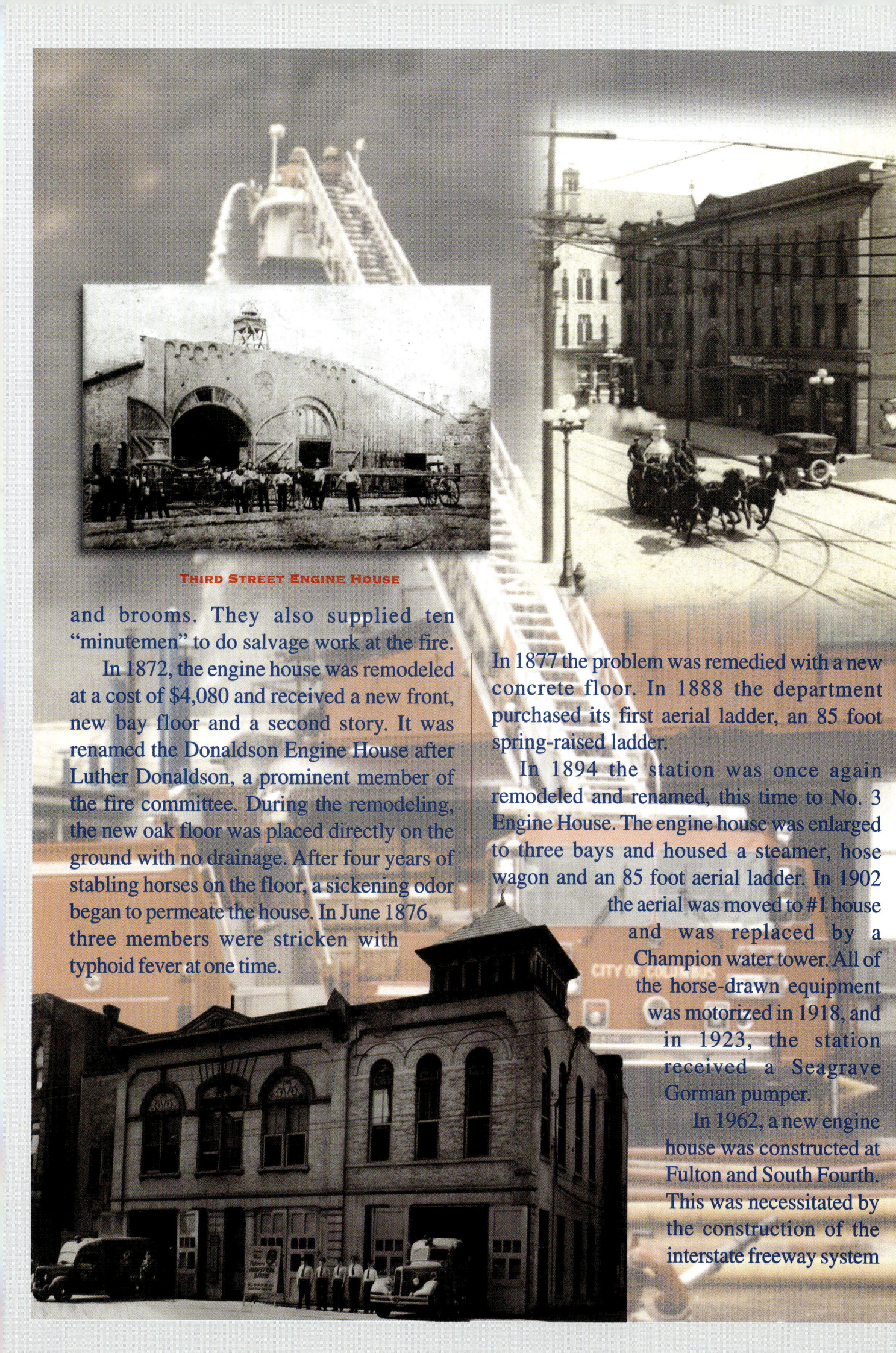

In 1962, a new engine house was constructed at Fulton and South Fourth. This was necessitated by the construction of the interstate freeway system and the Market-Mohawk redevelopment project. The equipment from Engine House 3 was combined with Engine House 2's equipment as a matter of economics, since the original engine houses were only a few blocks apart. Each engine has its own response area, Engine 2 responds south and Engine 3 responds north of the engine house.

A Columbus fire station had occupied the Third and Chapel location for 107 years. In December 1962, old engine house 2 and 3 were vacated and combined in the new station named Station #2.

Opened in December 1962, Station 2 is a one-story station with apparatus bays in the center and living quarters on the ends. The equipment responds to downtown Columbus and the surrounding freeway system. Station 2 also houses Heavy Rescue #2, one of the busiest rescues in the country. Bomb Squad 2 also is housed here, one of the very few fire department operated Bomb Squads in the nation. Equipment responding from Station #2 includes two engines, an aerial ladder with bucket, a Battalion Chief, a Rescue, the Bomb Squad and a Medic.

Station Four

O riginally located at Spruce and N. High Street, Station 4 was built in 1874 at a cost of $8,000. In July of 1874, a newly organized steam engine company and hose reel moved into the new station. In October 1874, a ladder company named "Gift" was organized and added to the station.

A new, larger engine house was built in 1892 at Russell and Hamlet, just east of the original engine house. The station cost $18,000 and was a two-story brick station with three bays. Engine 4 ran from here until sometime in 1940 when the engine house was closed and the engine was moved to Engine House #16 at Chestnut and N. Fourth Street. It ran out of 16's for a year-and-a-half as a second engine.

CHARACTER

Engine 4 responding.

Ladder called "Gift"

Spruce & N. 4th Streets

Horse Stalls

Russell & Hamlet

70

The station was remodeled in 1941 by firefighters and donations from local citizens and reopened with Squad 2, the training academy and communications workshop. In 1945, Squad 2 was taken out of service due to manpower and the station ceased to have active firefighting companies responding from it. The station would continue to be used for a training academy, union meetings and practices for the Fireman's Minstrel Shows.

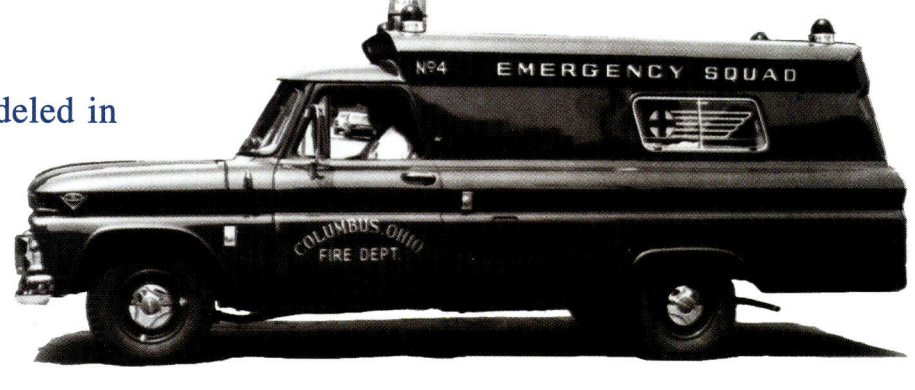

In 1952 the training academy was moved to Station 10. In 1957, Columbus annexed Marion Township and acquired a fire station at 2266 Lockbourne Road. It was a one-story, two-bay brick garage which housed the apparatus; and an adjacent schoolhouse 75 yards away which was converted into firefighter quarters. The station was designated Station 4 and on October 28, 1957, Engine 4 and new Squad 4 were placed in service. Tanker 4 replaced the squad at a later date. Crews ran from here until October 1975, when a new Station 4 was dedicated at 3030 Winchester Pike. The new station cost $426,000 and is a typical Columbus station with four bays, two on each end of the central living quarters.

In 1989, the Franklin County HAZMAT response vehicle was placed in service manned by Columbus Firefighters. Rescue 15 was moved to Station 4 and the Engine and Rescue were staffed with HAZMAT Personnel to establish a Hazardous Materials Response Team. Battalion Chief 4 was moved here around 1991, and a Medic vehicle was added with the departments' EMS/Paramedic system upgrade. Engine 4, Rescue 4 and Medic 4 respond as a combined unit with the county HAZMAT vehicle anywhere in Franklin County or to special calls outside the county.

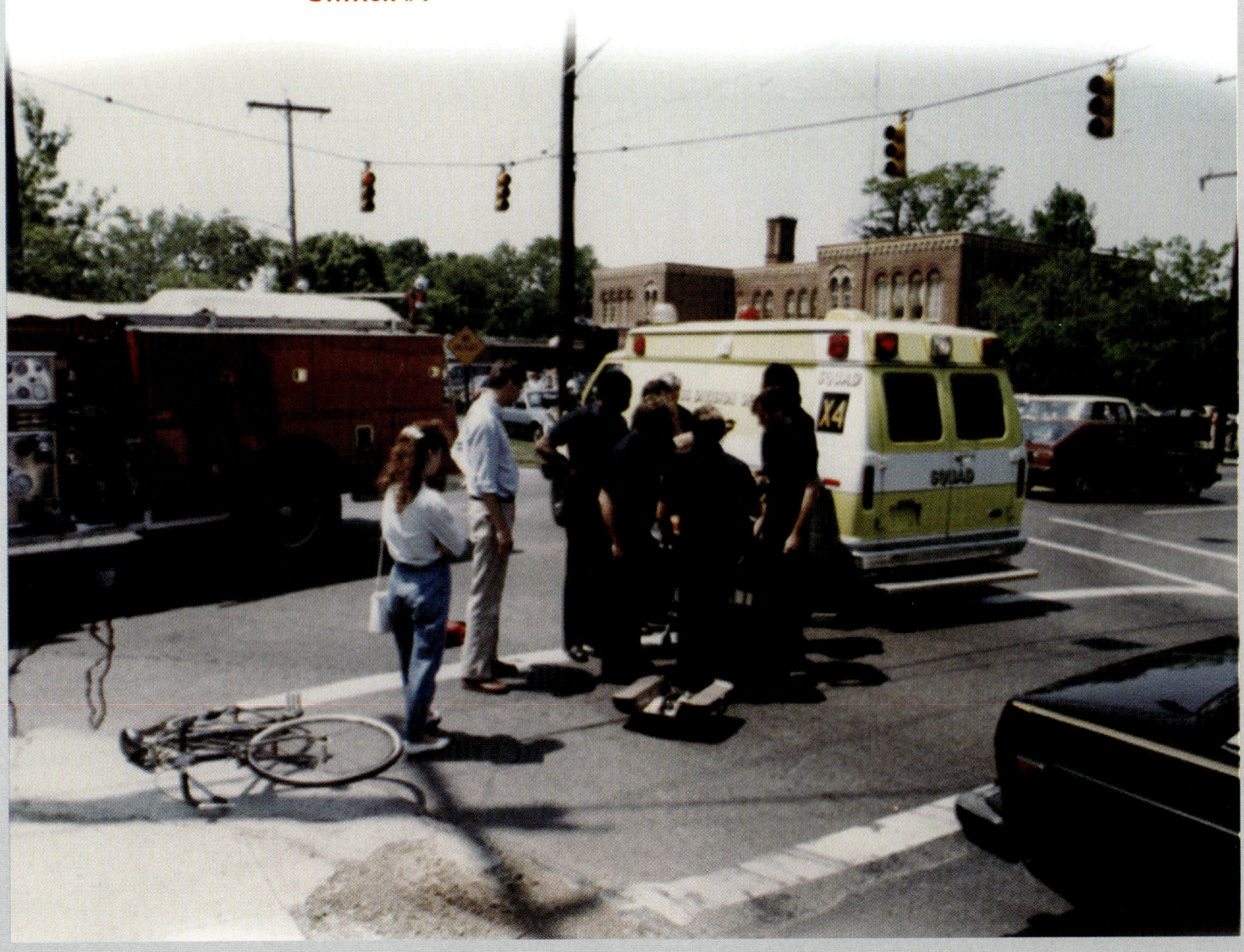

Station #4 — 2266 Lockborne Road

Station #4

Station Five

Station 5 was completed in 1892 at a cost of $15,000. The station was a brick three-story building with two bays. It included a large hose and bell tower. This was one of the first engine houses situated in a prominently residential area. The neighborhood was laid out and built by German immigrants and is still known as historic German Village. Most of the homes were small and very close together. The majority of streets in the area are still constructed of paving bricks.

The station was motorized in 1916, and in 1933 the floors were replaced with reinforced concrete and the bell tower was removed from the hose tower.

In 1968, the station was closed due to its proximity to other surrounding engine houses. It was also felt the manpower could be better utilized to man a ladder company in the south end, Ladder 22.

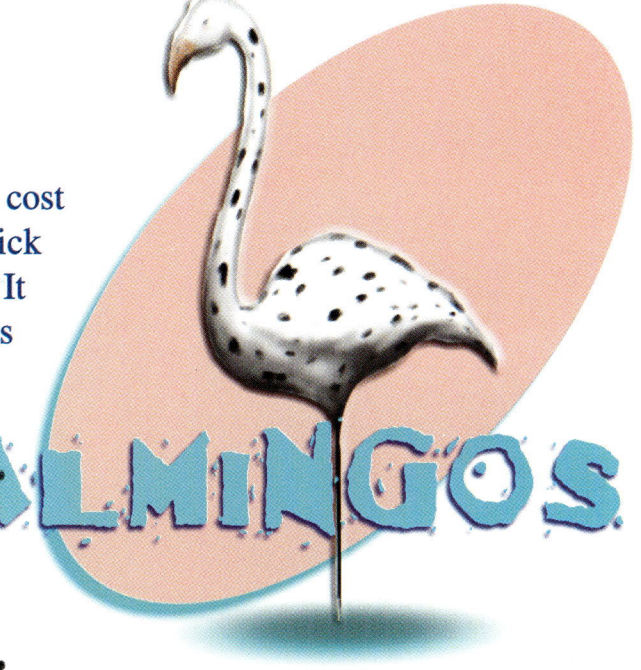

DALMINGOS

COMPASSION

121 Thurman Avenue

121 Thurman Avenue

A new Station 5 wouldn't be built until 1972. The station is located at 211 McNaughten Road on the Far East side of Columbus. It is a one-story brick building with two bays on each end of the central living quarters. The station cost $329,154 to build.

The old Engine House #5 was sold soon after its closing in 1968, and was restored and opened as a Seafood Restaurant featuring firehouse memorabilia. It is a favorite destination for local residents and fire service personnel.

OLD STATION #5 — THURMAN AVENUE

OLD STATION #5

75

Station Six

The first fire department building built west of the Scioto River was Hose House #6 at Mill and West Broad Street. It was built in 1880 at a cost of $2,650 and only housed a hose reel. The fire department had discontinued the use of steamers around this time in favor of hose reels. The hose from the reel was laid from the hydrant to the fire then the existing water pressure from the fire hydrant was used to fight the fire. However, water pressure varied greatly from area to area and fell drastically during heavy use times of day.

In 1890, the fire department returned to the use of steamers, which necessitated tearing down the small hose house and rebuilding a full-size engine house that would accommodate a steamer and horses.

COMPETENCE

MILL & WEST BROAD STREET

Work began on the new #6 engine house in 1891, and was completed in 1892. The engine house cost $13,940 and was a two bay, three-story brick station with a hose and bell tower. A steamer and hose reel were quartered here when opened. The steamer had a three-horse hitch and the horses' names were Tom, Piffie, and Baldy.

The station was closed in 1966 due to its proximity to Stations 10 and 17. These three stations, all located on West Broad Street, are perfect examples of how engine houses were situated during the horse-drawn era. The horses could pull the heavy steamers for about five blocks before starting to tire. Each of these engine houses are approximately ten blocks apart, therefore each stations' horses only had to run 5 blocks in each direction to maximize their effort. When the equipment was motorized this five-block standard was unnecessary and many engine houses were closed because they were to close to each other. The station still stands and has housed an electronics store since it's closing around 1966.

The current Station #6 was built in 1970 at a cost of $286,000. It is located at 5750 Maple Canyon Avenue at Dublin-Granville Road. It is a one-story brick building with three bays, one bay north of the central living quarters and two on the south. An Engine, Battalion Chief and a Medic respond out of this station to a heavy concentration of residential and commercial areas.

MILL & WEST BROAD STREET

"Smokey" the Fire Dog

Maple Canyon Avenue & Dublin Granville Road

78

Station Seven

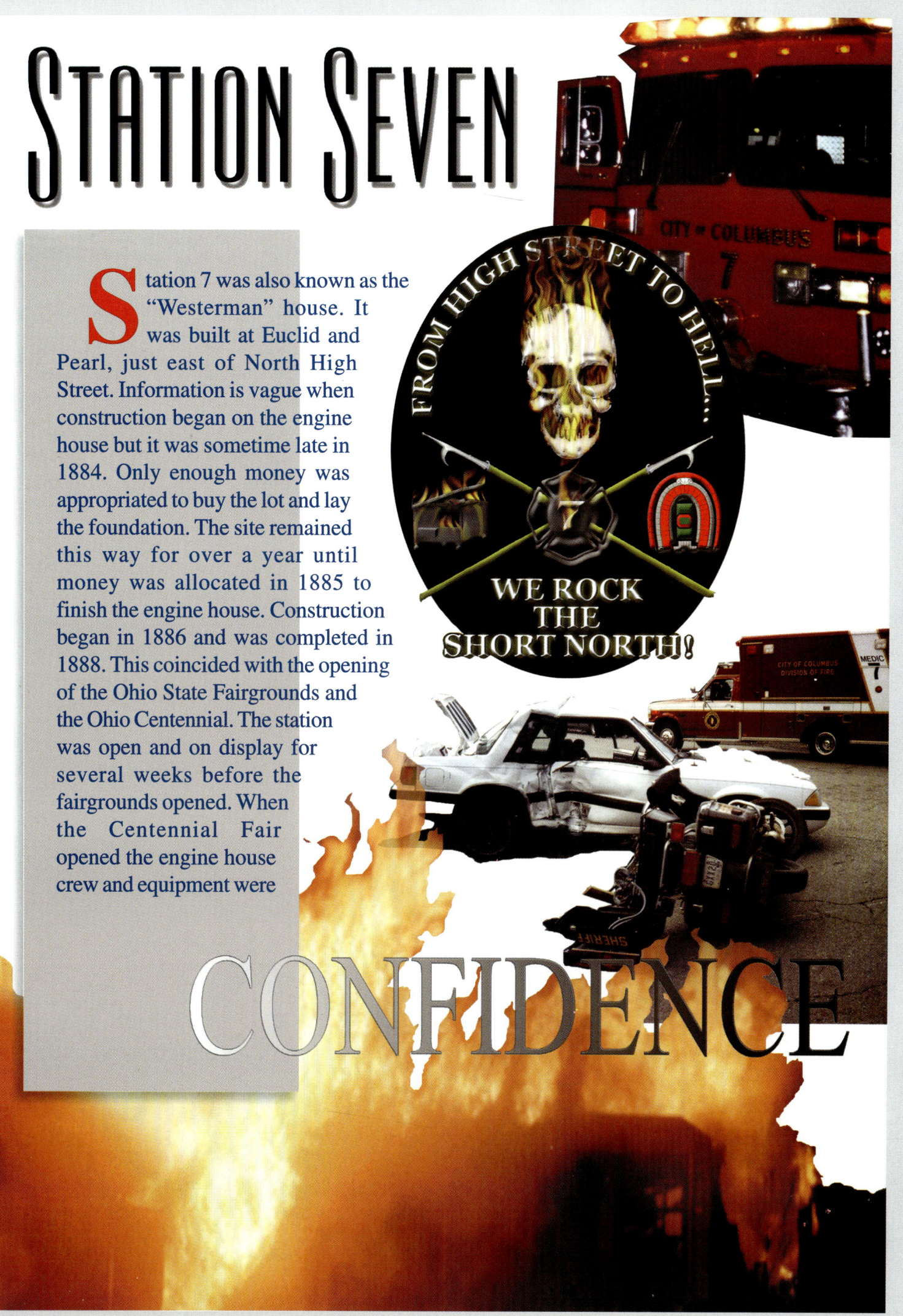

Station 7 was also known as the "Westerman" house. It was built at Euclid and Pearl, just east of North High Street. Information is vague when construction began on the engine house but it was sometime late in 1884. Only enough money was appropriated to buy the lot and lay the foundation. The site remained this way for over a year until money was allocated in 1885 to finish the engine house. Construction began in 1886 and was completed in 1888. This coincided with the opening of the Ohio State Fairgrounds and the Ohio Centennial. The station was open and on display for several weeks before the fairgrounds opened. When the Centennial Fair opened the engine house crew and equipment were

FROM HIGH STREET TO HELL...
WE ROCK THE SHORT NORTH!

CONFIDENCE

1425 INDIANOLA AVENUE

assigned to duty on the fairgrounds until the fair was over. They then returned to their new engine house on Euclid.

When opened in 1888, Engine House 7 was supplied with a new hose reel at a cost of $700. By 1890, steamers were being returned to use in Columbus and 7's was eventually so equipped. The steamer horses were named Shiner and Bud. The hose reel had a matched team of black horses named Jack and Ham. During a fire run, Jack slipped on a streetcar rail, slid against a curb and broke his right foreleg. He had to be "put down" and firefighters department-wide mourned the loss of one of their best friends.

The current Station 7 was opened on April 1, 1966 at 1425 Indianola Avenue. The station is located one block east of North High Street off of Eighth Avenue southeast of the Ohio State University campus. The brick station is one-story, with four bays: two bays on each end of the central living quarters. When opened, the fire department print shop and mask repair facility were located in the basement. The print shop was eventually closed and mask repair was moved to the basement of the shop on Greenlawn Avenue. Basic EMS and Paramedic classes were also taught in the basement of Station 7 for years.

Station 7 responds to high-density student housing, including numerous high-rise dormitories. The area also has various labs, sports arenas, research facilities and hospitals in the immediate vicinity.

The station motto is "From High Street To Hell-We Rock The Short North". The station is also affectionately known as "The Rock".

"THE ROCK" EUCLID AND PEARL

Station Eight

Station 8 was started in 1884, but only enough money was appropriated to buy the land and lay the foundation. The station was completed in 1885 and was located near the intersection of Mt. Vernon and Twentieth Street. It was a two-story, two-bay station with a hose and bell tower in the middle of the building. A horse drawn steamer and hose reel responded from this station until 1913, when motorized equipment was added.

A new station was built in 1968, several blocks east of the old station, at 1240 E. Long Street and N. Champion Avenue. It cost $265,446 and is a one-story brick station, with living quarters in the center and three apparatus bays on the ends; one on the east side and two on the west side. This was the basic design for many engine houses in Columbus and incorporated many firefighter ideas and innovations.

The 1884, station "No. 8" stone plaque was saved and is set in the wall of the Long Street station in the west bay. The original station was renovated and incorporated into a shopping plaza at 20th and Mt. Vernon. It is currently used as a childcare facility.

The station motto is "Firefightin' Eights" and uses a logo of a black eight ball on its apparatus.

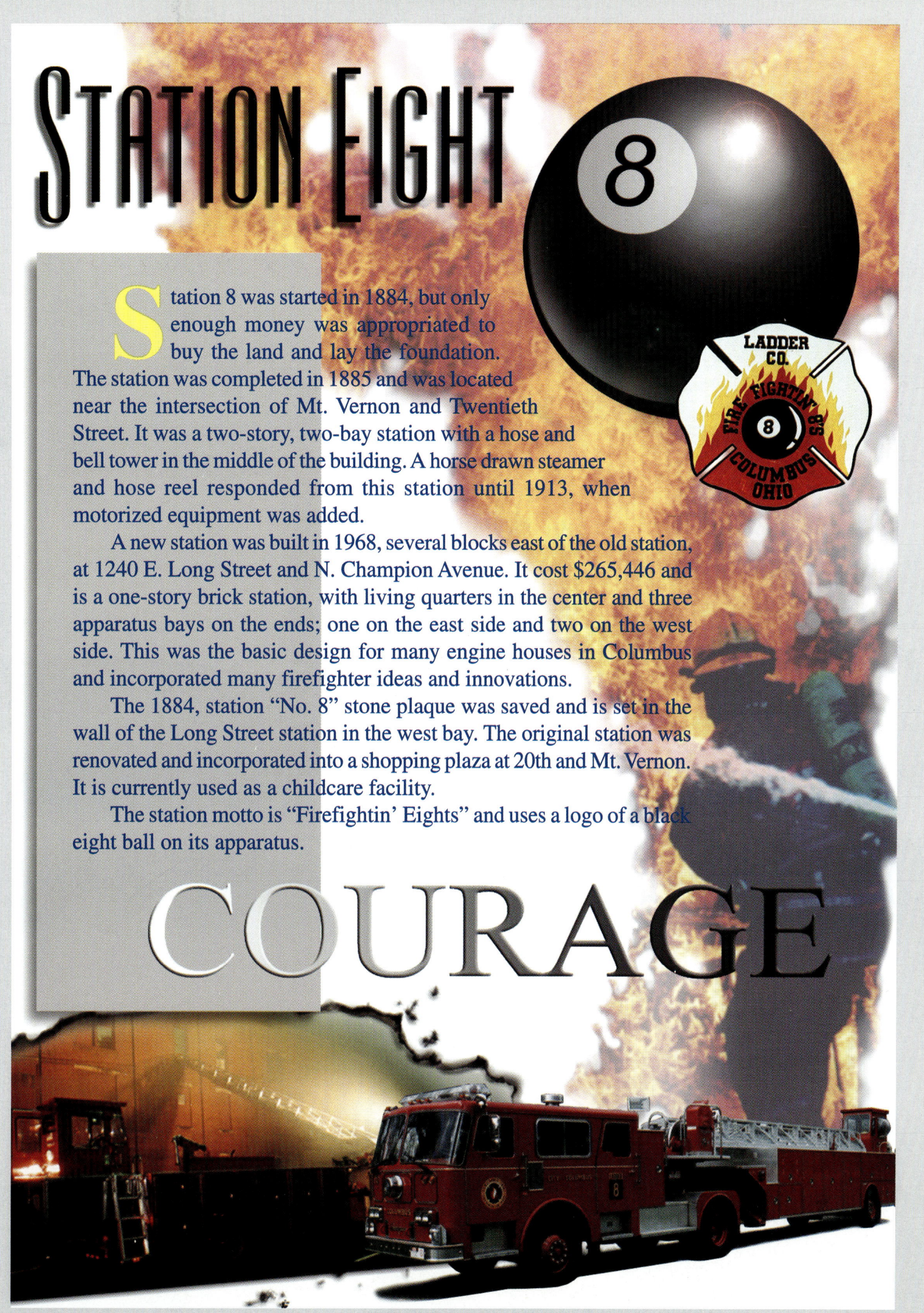

COURAGE

Stone originally located on 1885 Station is now located in current station.

Mt. Vernon & 20th

82

Mt. Vernon & 20th

1240 E. Long Street

83

84

Station Nine

Located in the "Flytown" area, Station 9 was built at Buttles and Delaware. The nickname "Flytown" arose because the area was growing so fast that the houses seemed to "fly up" overnight. The station was built in 1892 and cost $15,000. It was a three-story, two-bay brick station with a hose and bell tower.

During this time Columbus was returning to the use of steamers, having dropped their use in favor of using hand lines laid from hydrants and operating only off of available hydrant pressure.

DARING

The station opened in 1892 with a chemical wagon and a hose company, and received a steamer in 1894. All equipment here was horse-drawn until 1916 when the steamer received a Seagrave tractor. The station eventually had to be relocated due to the Goodale Redevelopment project. A new station was built in 1961 and the old station was torn down.

New Station 9 was located at 739 West Third Avenue, just west of the Olentangy River. It cost $157,647 and had two bays centrally located with living quarters on the two ends. Adjacent to the station is the Columbus Police Heliport and the police S.W.A.T. team facility.

Engine 9 responded to the University area, the nearby Olentangy River, residential areas and many shopping and commercial complexes in the area. Engine 9 was stationed here from 1961 until 1982. At that time, it was moved to new Station 1 at Naghten and North Fourth Street to complete Task Force 1 configuration of two engines and one ladder.

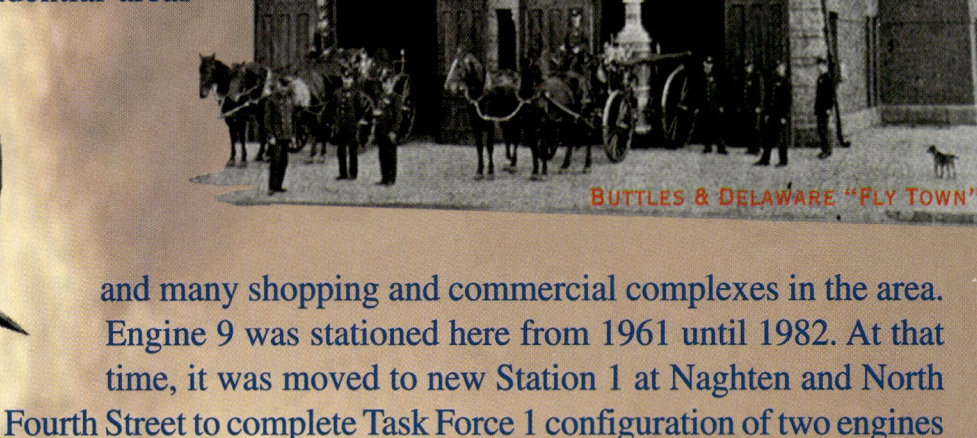

The West Third Avenue station was then converted into the Medical Training Center (MTC). It housed the offices of the Medical Director, the Training Nurse, the EMS Chief and EMS Supervisor. It also had classrooms for EMS training, storage for all EMS supplies and extra EMS vehicles. The MTC operated at this location from 1982 until 1995 when the new Fire Training and Administrative Complex opened on Parsons Avenue.

The station opened once again as an active engine house in July 1995, renamed Station 25. This replaced a closed Station 25 that had been located at Port Columbus International Airport. The station was closed when Crash/Rescue services were changed to a private company.

Engine 9 continues to respond from Station 1 located in the downtown Columbus area. It is co-located with Engine and Ladder 1, Medic 1, EMS Supervisor 11, the Safety Officer and the on-duty emergency services chief.

BUTTLES & DELAWARE "FLY TOWN"

Station Ten

Station 10 is located at 1096 W. Broad Street, in an area known as "the bottoms". It was built in 1897 at the intersection of Glenwood and W. Broad and cost $22,139 to build. This included the horses, harnesses, furnishings, hose and apparatus. It is a two-story, three-bay station with a hose and bell tower.

In 1933, a reinforced concrete floor was installed and the top part of the hose tower was removed down to the deck below the bell.

The Training Academy was located here from 1952, until the new Greenlawn Avenue Training Academy opened in 1962.

The firefighters stationed here refer to themselves as the "River Rats" and have a "River Rat" character logo for the station and apparatus. The River Rat nickname refers to the time of the 1913 flood when the river literally flooded the station.

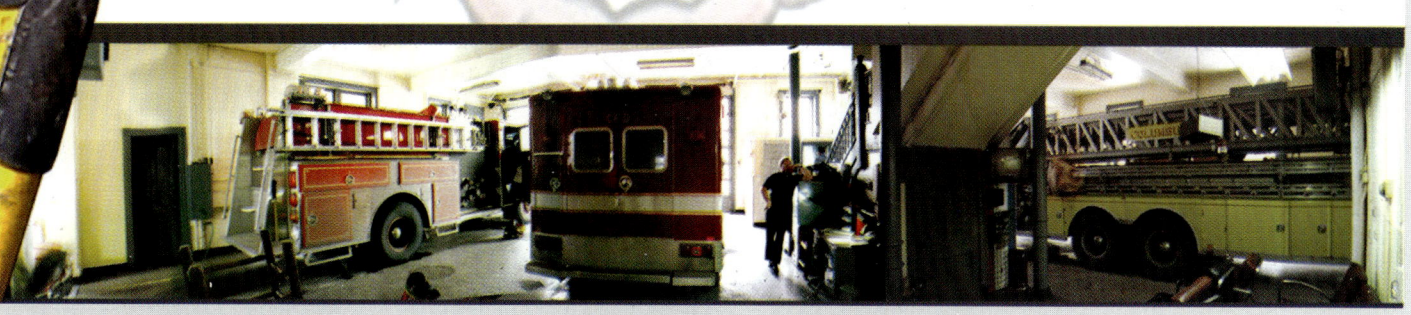

DEDICATION

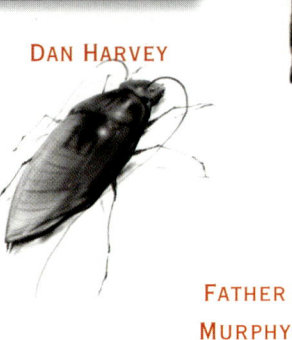

1096 W. Broad Street

Dan Harvey

Father Murphy

The station has caught on fire twice over the years. The first was a kitchen fire caused by a gas stove, which occurred in 1971.

The second occurred on January 15, 1976, when an accidental fire on the second floor caused about $6,000 damage. The station was not damaged enough to take it out of service, but was embarrassing to the men on duty.

The station has long needed replacement but a new station cannot be constructed until a floodwall for the area is completed. Land adjacent to the station has been purchased for a new station and will be constructed similar to the current Station 17 located west of 10's.

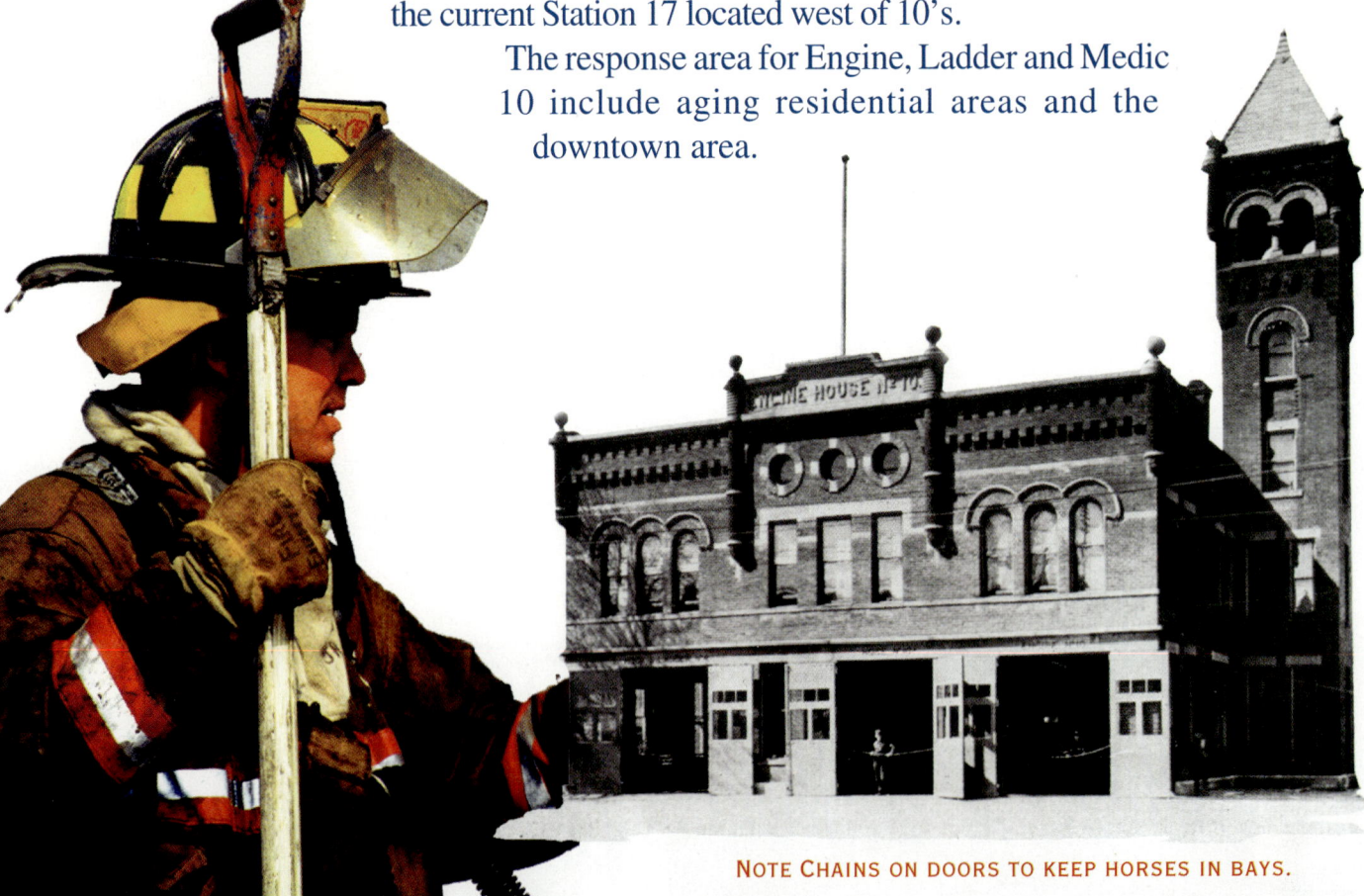

The response area for Engine, Ladder and Medic 10 include aging residential areas and the downtown area.

Note Chains on doors to keep horses in bays.

89

90

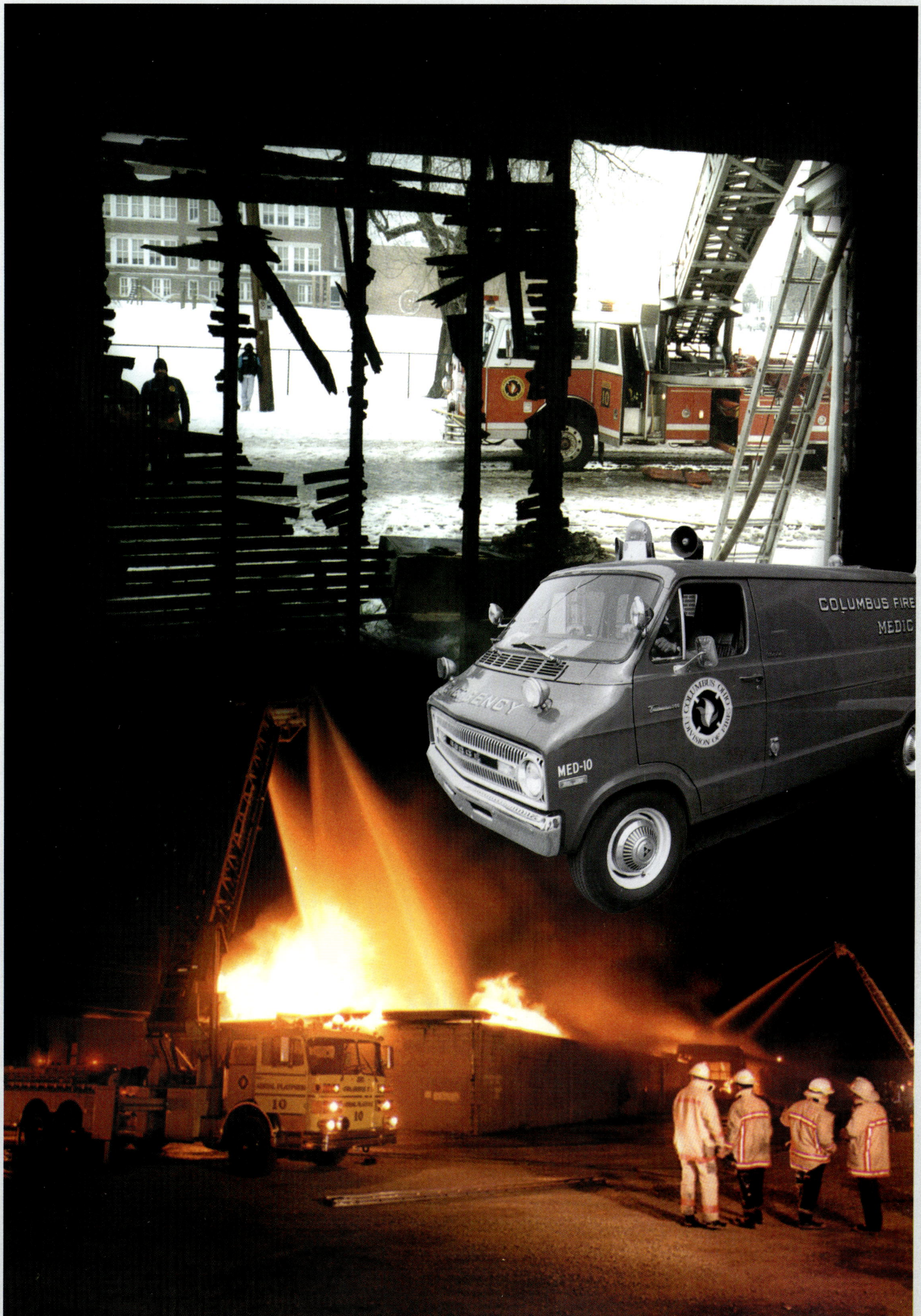
COLUMBUS FIRE
MEDIC
MED-10

BILL SEESHOLTZ LAST DAY.

Station Eleven

The first Station 11 was built in 1897 at E. Main Street and Twenty-second Street. It cost $12,863 to build and an additional $10,790 for equipment and furnishings. It was a three-bay station with a hose and bell tower. After a recommendation by the 1963 National Board of Fire Underwriters, Station 11 was closed in February 1970. It was purchased in 1999 to be used as a community outreach center.

Six months later, under an agreement with the fire department and Ohio State University, a new Station 11 was placed in service at Don Scott (OSU) Airport in northwest Columbus. On July 10, 1970, Engine 11 moved into an OSU provided building to provide crash/rescue service to the airport; and at the same time increased fire protection to the rapidly expanding northwest area at minimal cost to both parties.

OHIO STATE BATTALION No. 7
ENGINE 11 RESCUE
AIRCRASH 1
MEDIC & EMS 17
UNIVERSITY AIRPORT

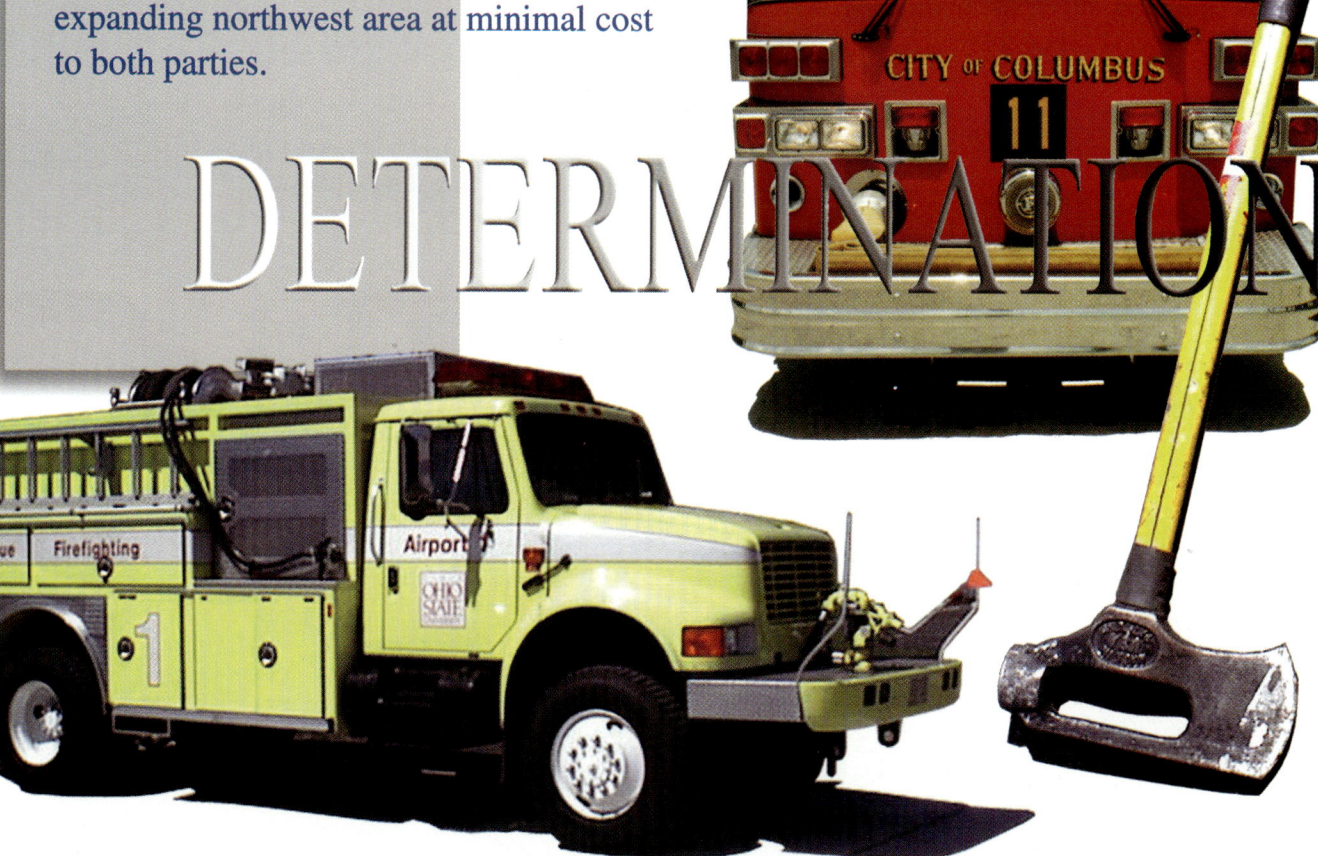

DETERMINATION

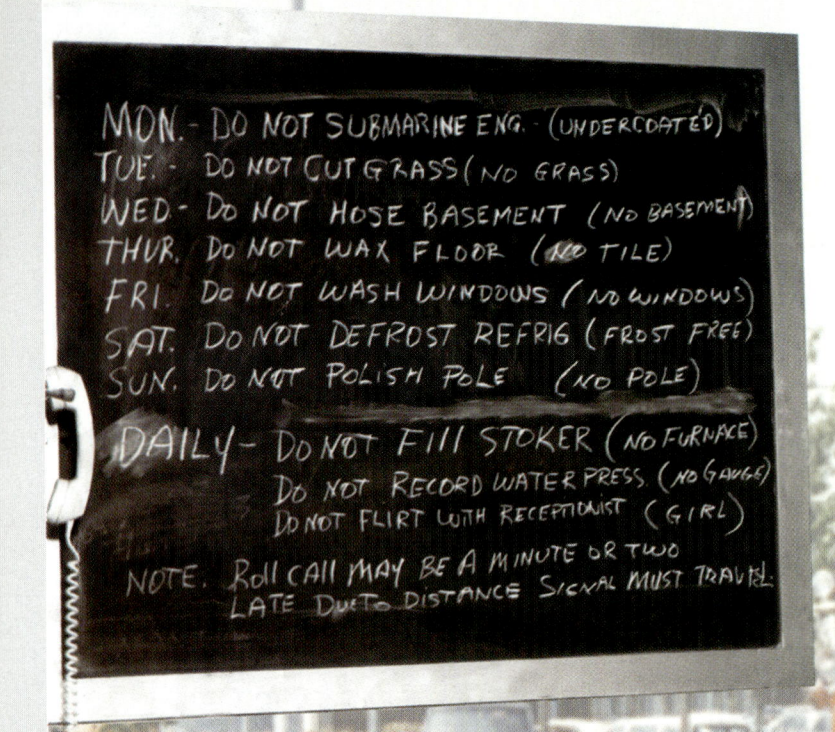

MON. - DO NOT SUBMARINE ENG. (UNDERCOATED)
TUE. - DO NOT CUT GRASS (NO GRASS)
WED - DO NOT HOSE BASEMENT (NO BASEMENT)
THUR. DO NOT WAX FLOOR (NO TILE)
FRI. DO NOT WASH WINDOWS (NO WINDOWS)
SAT. DO NOT DEFROST REFRIG (FROST FREE)
SUN. DO NOT POLISH POLE (NO POLE)

DAILY- DO NOT FILL STOKER (NO FURNACE)
DO NOT RECORD WATER PRESS. (NO GAUGE)
DO NOT FLIRT WITH RECEPTIONIST (GIRL)

NOTE. Roll call may be a minute or two late due to distance signal must travel.

As the northwest area of the city grew and the airport increased in size and air traffic it became apparent that a new station was needed. An agreement was reached that allowed Columbus to build a new station on leased OSU property. Construction began on the station in 1990 and the station opened January 27, 1992.

It is located at 2200 W. Case Road at the intersection of Dierker Road and cost $1.1 million to build. It is built on the same plans and was constructed at the same time as Station 32. This is a design that provides individual bedrooms and restrooms to accommodate female firefighters. The design was improved over the previous Station 30 and 31 by adding full basements and larger dining and living areas. The old OSU provided building had 1000 square feet of living space, compared with the new stations' 4900 square feet.

Station 11 was also slightly modified to house a rescue and new Battalion Chief for the fast growing northwest area. OSU also supplies a crash truck for the airfield that is staffed by the firefighters of Station 11. Engine 11, Rescue 11, Medic 11, Battalion 7 and EMS 17 respond from this location. The station is a one-story building with living quarters centrally located and two bays on each end. The airport crash truck responds out the back of the station directly onto the field.

As the northwest area continues to grow so have the number of responses by Engine 11. In the year 2000, Engine 11 had just over 2000 runs, the most runs in the history of the engine company. The addition of Medic 11 in 1999 provided additional Emergency Medical Service to the northwest quadrant. The Medic units' runs also continue to increase. It currently averages five to six runs per day.

2200 W. Case Road

Station Twelve

In 1880, a Hose House was built for hose reel #5 at a cost of $3,180. The house was located at Oak Street and Marble Alley, and the hose reel was manned by all black firefighters. In 1892, the house was remodeled to accommodate a chemical engine and was re-designated Chemical House #1. The crew was still an all black crew. In 1896, the crew and equipment were moved to a temporary location at 18th and Oak while the station was totally rebuilt.

In 1897, the new larger engine house was opened as Engine House 12. The new station cost $16,385, including the equipment, horses and furnishings. The station was a brick three-story station with two bays, with a hose and bell tower. A new Ahrens steamer and a combination chemical and hose wagon were stationed here.

STATION TWELVE
CAMP CHASE
ENGINE 12
12TH CAVALRY
LADDER 12
BEST IN THE WEST
1861   1865
ENGINE   LADDER   MEDIC

"The Dirty Dozen"

DEVOTION

In 1947, a forty-hour week was instituted and Engine 12 was taken out of service due to lack of manpower. During 1944, a fire squad (forerunner of our EMS system) was stationed here and ran from here until 1952, when the station was closed.

There would be no Engine 12 from 1947 until March 1, 1952, when new Station 12 opened at Brinker and Sullivant. The station had been built to be 22's, but was designated 12's to fill the gap in the numbering system. The station cost $132,566 and is located at 3200 Sullivant Avenue on the west side of Columbus. A ladder company was moved here from 17's in 1966.

Station 12 responds to residential areas, a large tank farm complex, large shopping mall complexes and industrial complexes. They also respond on mutual aid with Franklin Township.

Old Station 12 at Oak and Marble has been renovated and houses a party house and music hall.

97

Station Thirteen

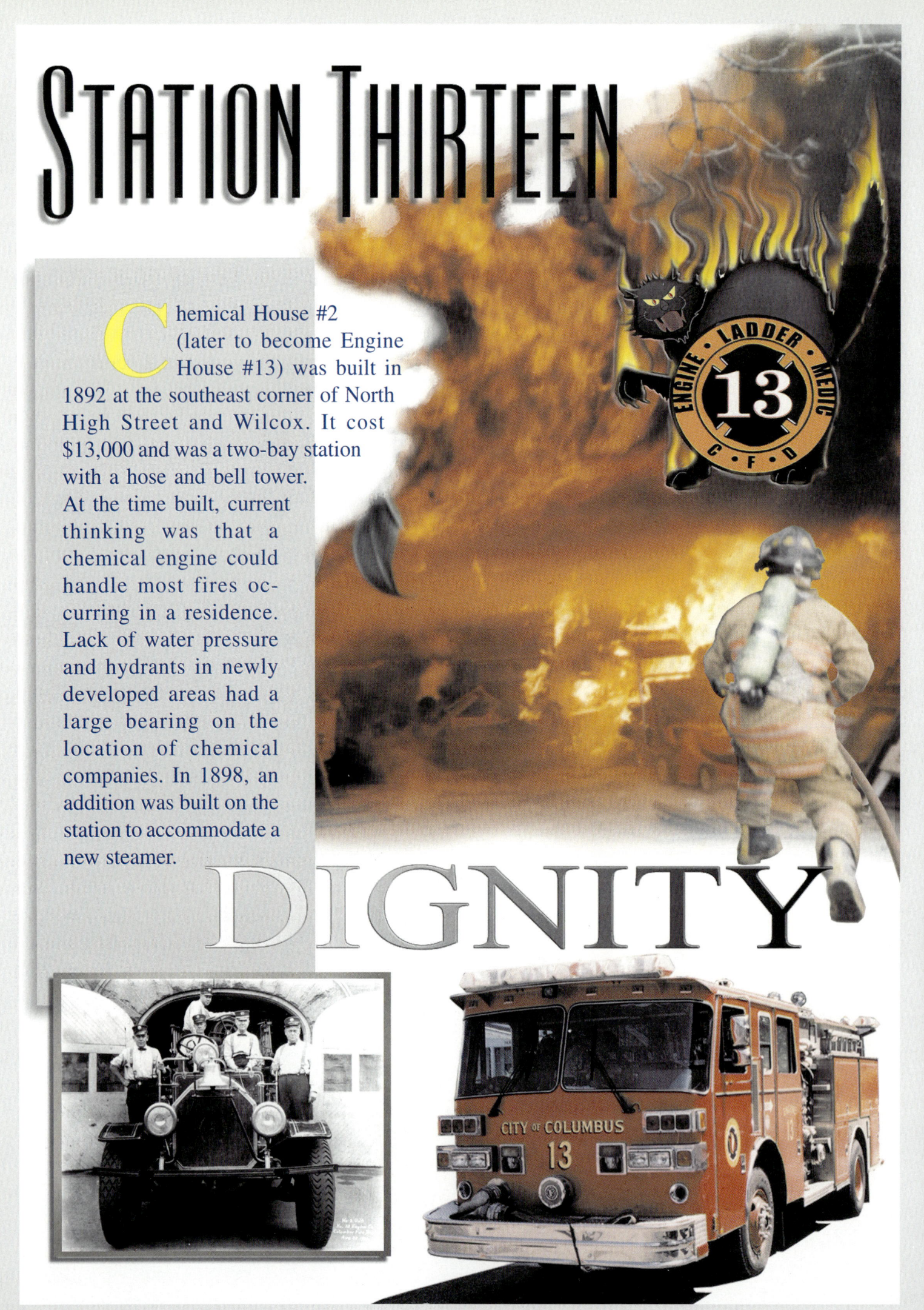

Chemical House #2 (later to become Engine House #13) was built in 1892 at the southeast corner of North High Street and Wilcox. It cost $13,000 and was a two-bay station with a hose and bell tower. At the time built, current thinking was that a chemical engine could handle most fires occurring in a residence. Lack of water pressure and hydrants in newly developed areas had a large bearing on the location of chemical companies. In 1898, an addition was built on the station to accommodate a new steamer.

DIGNITY

A new station was constructed and dedicated September 1, 1957. It is located at Arcadia and Deming Avenue and cost $178,000. It is a brick one-story station with two apparatus bays in the center and living quarters on the sides. It responds to a mix of residential, commercial and light industrial areas, including the Ohio State University.

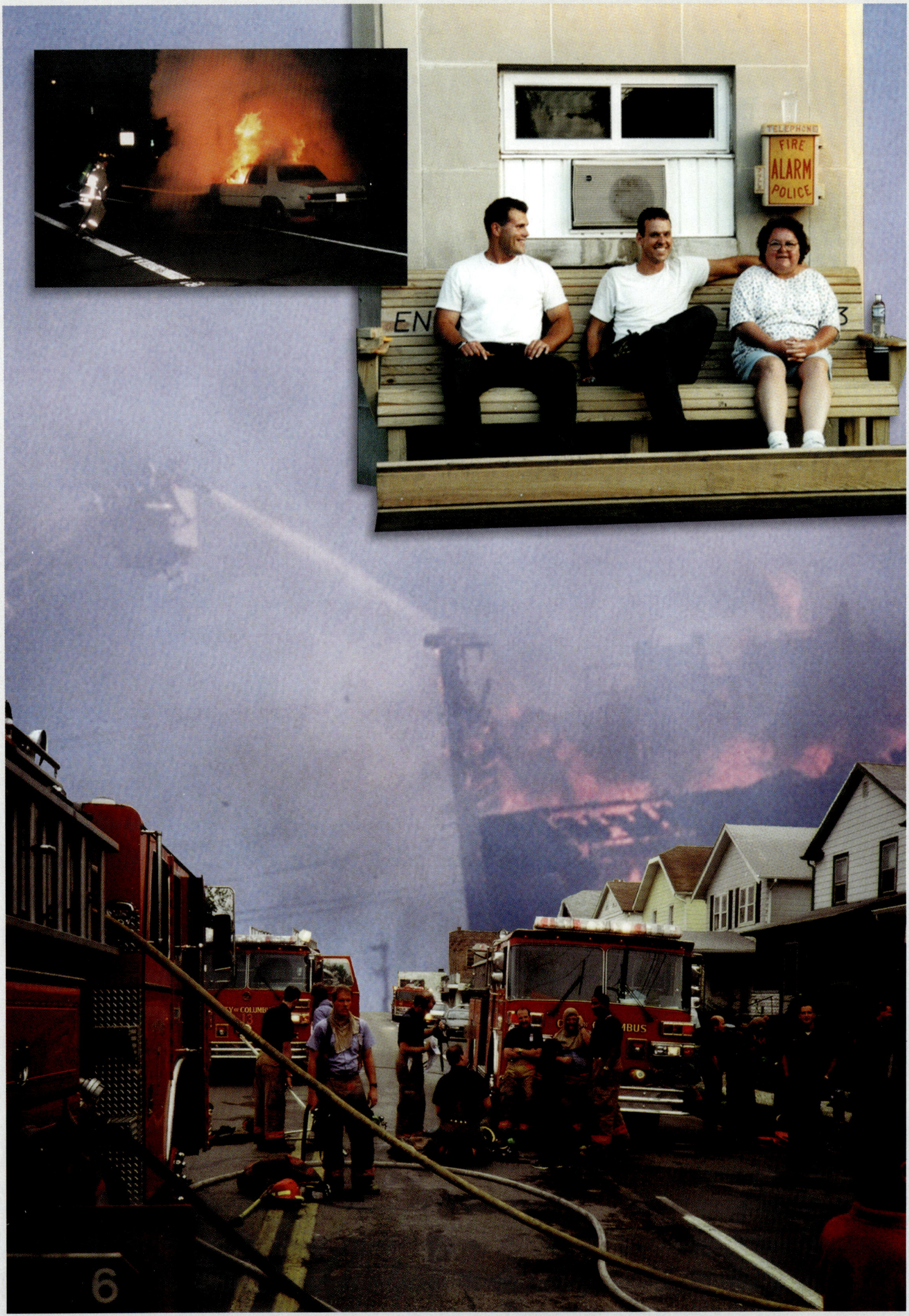
TELEPHONE
FIRE
ALARM
POLICE

Station Fourteen

Station 14 was built in 1906, and is located at 1716 Parsons Avenue, at the intersection of Hinman and Parsons. At that time Hinman was called McCort Street. The station cost $14,285 and was originally a brick three-story station with a hose and bell tower. In 1913, a reinforced concrete floor was installed and in 1916, all equipment was motorized.

In 1956, a second engine, called 14A, responded from 14's until moved to Station 4 on Lockbourne Road. Station 4 was a station annexed from Marion Township and Engine 14A moved there in 1957, and became Engine 4. A squad was also stationed there at this time.

In 1959, Squad 4 moved to Station 14 and become Squad 14. In 1973, a third bay was added to the station to house a ladder company. Ladder 22 from Southgate and Parsons, south of 14's, was moved in for better coverage of the south end and to be closer to downtown.

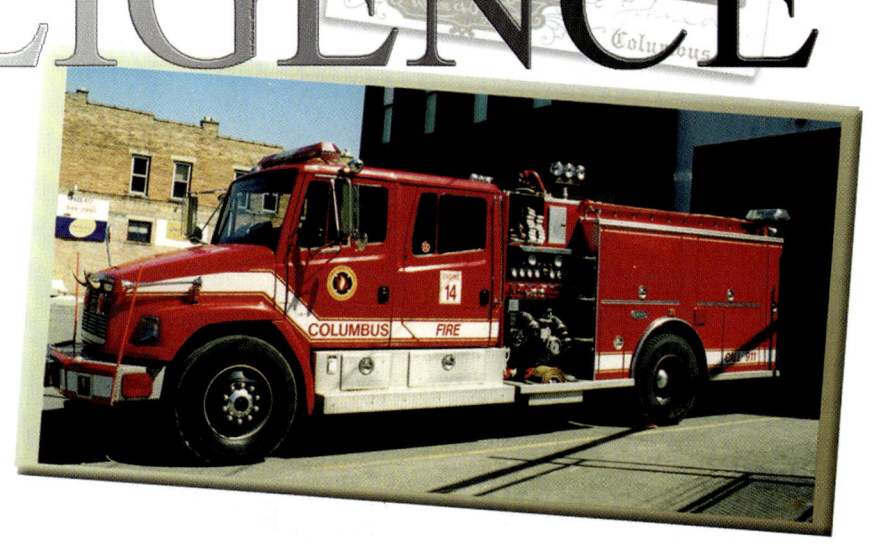

ELVIS
"North Graceland"

DILIGENCE

Around 1991, the station adopted "Elvis" as their station mascot and became Columbus' "Graceland". Of course, the obligatory velvet Elvis is hanging prominently in the front window of the apparatus bay along with other unique Elvis memorabilia donated to the station over the years. This has made visits to Station 14 very enjoyable for all Elvis fans young and old.

A new two-story station was occupied in 2001. It is located north of the current station at 1514 Parsons Avenue at the intersection of Jenkins Avenue. The station crew is attempting to rename a short section of Jenkins from Parsons to the alley at the rear of the station "Elvis Presley Boulevard".

There are no current plans for the 1906 station when vacated.

103

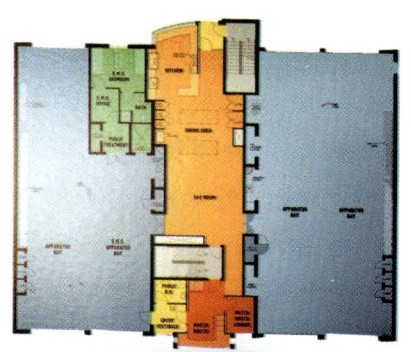

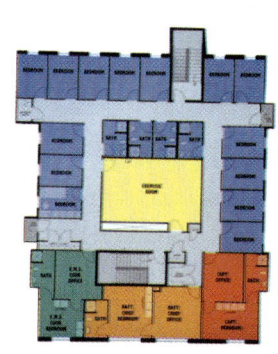

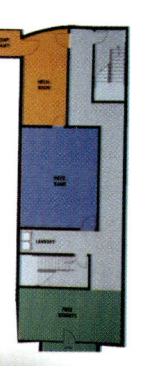

Station Fifteen

Station 15 was constructed in 1907 at 640 E. Livingston Avenue at Ann Street. It cost $20,000 to build, with the land costing $2,750. It was a three-story brick building with a hose and bell tower and three apparatus bays. This would be the next to last station built to house horses and have a barn and hayloft. It was a twin to Station 16, with the exception of the towers being on opposite sides.

The station had a dog mascot, "Jackie". Each week, a neighbor would leave a full fresh bag of Bull-Durham chewing tobacco for Jackie as a treat.

DUTY

1800 E. LIVINGSTON AVENUE

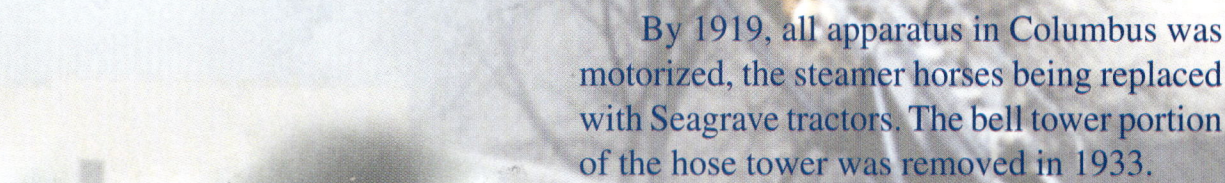

By 1919, all apparatus in Columbus was motorized, the steamer horses being replaced with Seagrave tractors. The bell tower portion of the hose tower was removed in 1933.

In 1963, a National Board of Underwriters Report recommended relocating 15's farther east. By 1969 the move to a new station at 1800 E. Livingston Avenue was completed.

The new station is located at E. Livingston and Rhoades and was dedicated March 12, 1969. It was built at a cost of $234,075 and is a one-story brick station. It has central living quarters and three apparatus bays.

105

Station Sixteen

Station 16 was built in 1908, at 260 N. Fourth Street. It cost $28,672 to construct and is located at the intersection of Chestnut and N. Fourth. It is situated on three parcels of land that originally cost $25,670. It is a three-story brick building with a hose and bell tower and three apparatus bays. It was the last station built in Columbus to house horses, which included a barn and hayloft. The department became fully motorized on December 27, 1919, with the retirement of steamer 16's three-horse team. The horses were three grays named Bill, Jim and Rex. A Seagrave tractor replaced the last horse team in the department.

EFFORT

In 1912, a shop building was constructed at the rear of Station 16. It housed the maintenance shop, a cistern for pump testing and the communications supply shop.

The station was renamed Station 1 in 1953, when a new Station 16 was opened. The department was filling a gap in the numbering system since there was no Station 1 at this time, and #1 was traditionally a downtown station.

The current Station 16 is located at Weber and McGuffey. It cost $137,674 to build and opened on June 14, 1953. It was the first engine house built in the north end in over twenty years. Until 24's opened in 1960, Ladder 16's longest run north was seven miles, "as the crow flies". The same length run to the south would have passed seven engine houses and three other ladder companies.

260 N. 4th Street

It is located on the northeast side of Columbus and responds to primarily residential areas. The station is brick with two bays in the middle with living quarters on the sides. An Engine, Rescue and Medic currently respond out of this station.

The original 1908 station remained Station 1 from 1953 until 1981 when a new Station 1 was built one block away. A non-profit group of firefighters saved the building in 1983 by procuring a ninety-nine year lease to build and operate a fire museum and fire prevention center.

The building was renamed Engine House #16 and totally restored to its original appearance in 1990. The building is currently on the City of Columbus Historic Register and has been placed on the National Register of Historic Places. It is currently undergoing a first floor renovation to begin teaching fire prevention with a scheduled opening in mid 2002.

Rescue No. 16 Business

Rescue No. 16 Fun

Weber & McGuffey

108

Station Seventeen

Keepers of the Hill 17

In 1897, Chemical House #1 was constructed at West Broad Street and Whitethorne Avenue. It cost $4,926 and was a wood frame one-bay, two-story building with a bell tower. When completed, the equipment and all black crew from Chemical House #1 at Oak and Marble were moved here. The station was occupied until early 1913, when a larger engine house was built. After it was closed, it was used as a temporary morgue and food distribution point during the flood of 1913.

The new station was located at West Broad and Wheatland, on State-owned property adjacent to the "asylum", and cost $19,858. The property was leased from the State for $1.00 a year for ninety-nine years. The station was located at 2300 W. Broad and was a brick, three-story, three-bay station with a hose and bell tower.

Endurance

It was the last engine house built during the horse-drawn era, but the first not built to house horses, which required a barn, stables and hayloft. Station 17 had the first gasoline-powered pumper in the department, a Seagrave turbine powered pumper. It is stated that the pumper could throw three streams of water over a ten-story building.

A new Station 17 was opened January 21, 1994 at 2250 W. Broad, next to its previous location. The station cost $1,308,000 and as before, the 1.4-acre property is leased from the State of Ohio for $1.00 a year. The station is a one-story brick building with living quarters in the center and two bays on each end. Located on a hill overlooking the "bottoms", the crew and station have been dubbed "Keepers of the Hill".

Engine, Rescue and Medic 17, as well as Battalion 5 and EMS 15, respond to an older residential and light commercial area on the west side of Columbus.

The old 1913 engine house is currently in use as a community center for the area.

Station Eighteen

The Knight's
Engine   Medic
of Windsor

Constructed in 1926, Station 18 is located at Cleveland Avenue and Windsor. It cost $39,495 to build and is a brick, two-bay, two-story station. A lot at Cleveland Avenue and Gibbard was originally purchased for the station. But when the Village of Linden was annexed a need was seen for an engine house farther north, that location being at Windsor.

In 1951, the department print shop was moved here. It remained until Station 7 was built in 1966 with a planned area for the print shop.

Due to its small size, apparatus has to be special ordered low and short to fit in the bays. Property has been purchased in the vicinity to build a new station and plans are to begin construction sometime in 2003 or 2004. The new station will be similar in design to the new two-story Station 14.

Engine and Medic 18 respond to primarily residential areas.

EXCELLENCE

111

Station Nineteen

Station 19, also known as the "Northmoor" engine house, was built in 1931. It cost $39,887 and is located at 3601 North High Street, at the intersection of Northmoor and N. High. It is a two-story, two-bay brick station.

It was the only station built during the depression and the last to be built for almost twenty years. It was started in March 1930 – five months after the stock market crash of 1929. It was built to blend in with the surrounding residential area. It blends in so well that firefighters sent to 19's for the first time drive by it without realizing it is an engine house.

Station 19 would be the last station built more than one-story tall and using brass poles for many years. It was felt that in terms of comfort, convenience and safety the one-floor engine house was a much better design. It would be fifty years

FORTITUDE

(1931-1982) before another Columbus fire station would have poles. This would be Station 1 in downtown Columbus, where property is at a premium and building "up" is necessary. Ironically, there is a pole from the third floor to the second, then three separate poles from the second floor to the first floor apparatus bays.

In 1931, the Northmoor Engine House was the far north end of Columbus. "First in" runs of five or six miles were not uncommon before Stations 24, 11, 6 and a mutual aid agreement with Sharon Township (Worthington) were completed.

The engine house is now too small for the larger engines and other fire equipment. Engines have to be special ordered short and low to fit in the stations small bays. Plans to replace the station have been on hold since 1975 over a land dispute. Property has now been purchased adjacent to the current station and a new station is planned for 2003 or 2004. Due to community efforts and input the new station will incorporate the original station in it's new design.

The station motto is "The Pride On High" and a Lion is the mascot logo. The primary response area is residential.

Station Twenty

The General

Station 20 was opened May 6, 1951 and cost $125,360. It is located at 2646 East Fifth Avenue at the intersection of Dawson and E. Fifth. Station 20 and 21 were the first engine houses of a new concept and design. They incorporated several modern improvements like rear apparatus doors to eliminate backing into the station and heated bay floors. The living quarters and apparatus are all on the first floor, seemingly spelling the end of the firemen's brass pole that caused numerous injuries. In terms of comfort, convenience and safety the one-floor engine house was a much better design. A station with a pole would not be built again until 1982 at Station 1.

Heroism

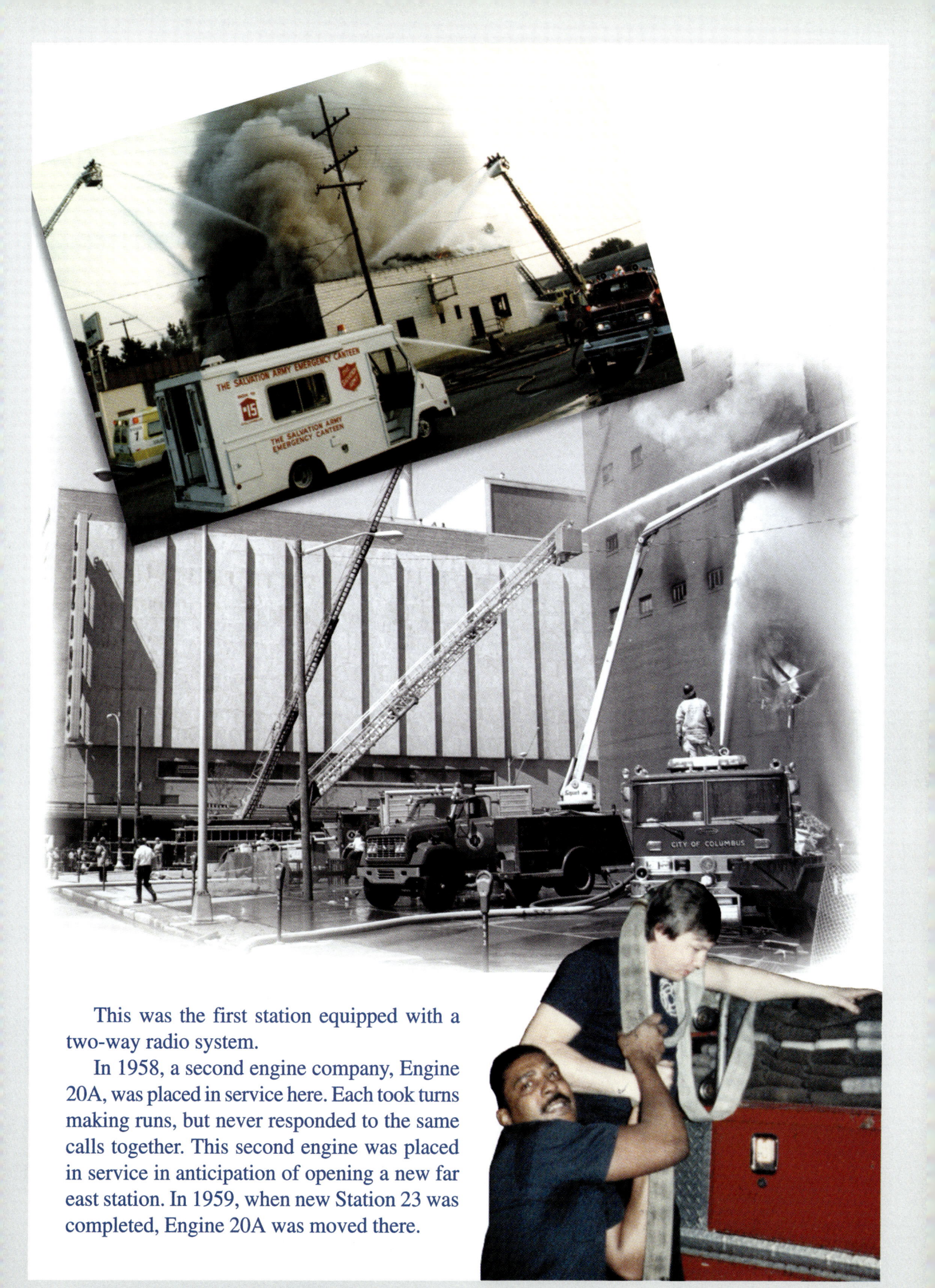

This was the first station equipped with a two-way radio system.

In 1958, a second engine company, Engine 20A, was placed in service here. Each took turns making runs, but never responded to the same calls together. This second engine was placed in service in anticipation of opening a new far east station. In 1959, when new Station 23 was completed, Engine 20A was moved there.

ENGINE HOUSE NUMBER 20

Station Twentyone

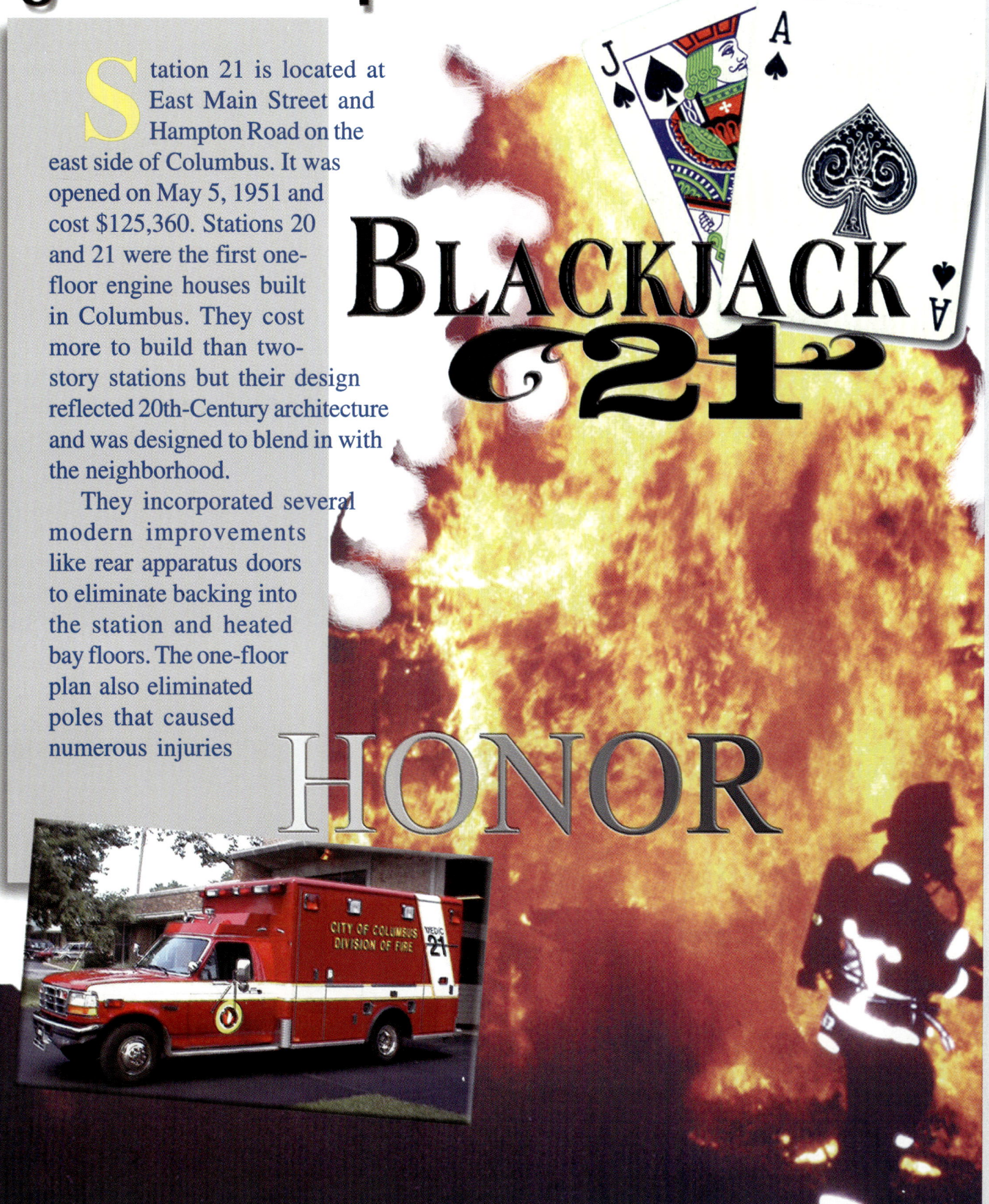

Station 21 is located at East Main Street and Hampton Road on the east side of Columbus. It was opened on May 5, 1951 and cost $125,360. Stations 20 and 21 were the first one-floor engine houses built in Columbus. They cost more to build than two-story stations but their design reflected 20th-Century architecture and was designed to blend in with the neighborhood.

They incorporated several modern improvements like rear apparatus doors to eliminate backing into the station and heated bay floors. The one-floor plan also eliminated poles that caused numerous injuries

Blackjack "21"

HONOR

and some early retirements because of permanent disabilities.

The station opened with the first two prototype Seagrave 70th Anniversary Edition fire trucks. Engine 21 and Ladder 21, a 65-foot aerial ladder, were the first engine and ladder of this new model built at the Columbus Seagrave plant in 1951. The ladder was moved to Station 23 in 1970 to give better coverage to the east side and Eastland Shopping Center.

Station 21 responds to residential areas, Port Columbus Airport, manufacturing and commercial complexes. It also responds by contract into the City of Bexley and has mutual aid with the City of Whitehall and the Defense Supply Construction Center.

Station Twentytwo

The southern most fire station in Columbus is Station 22 located at 3069 Parsons Avenue. It opened its doors for business in September 1959 and cost $147,860. The style of the building is typical of the stations built during this period. The two bays are located in the center with living quarters on both sides. Station 22 was the first engine house built in the southern portion of the city since #14 house was opened in 1906.

From September 1959 until 1969, only Engine 22 was stationed here. When Engine House #5 closed on Thurman Avenue in 1969, the crew was used to put a new ladder in service at 22's. The ladder ran from 22's until 1973, when an additional bay was put on Station 14. This gave the south end better coverage and put the ladder closer to the downtown area.

KINDNESS

Interestingly, current Station 12 on Sullivant Avenue has Station 22 on the dedication plaque. Old Station 12 on Oak Street was closed in 1947 due to lack of manpower when the new forty-hour workweek was implemented. When planned, the Sullivant Avenue station was to be #22, but when built in 1952, the department named it Station 12 to fill the gap in the numbering sequence. It would be seven more years before the current Station 22 would be built. A ladder was again stationed at 22's in the 1980's.

Engine, Ladder and Medic 22 respond to the Great Southern Shopping Center, Buckeye Steel Castings, heavy industries on Marion Road and large residential areas.

They respond on mutual aid with Hamilton Township and Rickenbacker Port Authority and airport.

1971 – Engines, Ladders, and Squads at 22's.
April 1973 – Squad moved to 14's
Fall 1973 – Ladder moved to 14's
1980s – Ladder put in service at 22's
November 1988 – Squad 14 moved to 22's
Spring 1996 – Squad 22 changed to Medic 22

Station Twentythree

Built in 1959, Station 23 is located at Hamilton Road and East Livingston Avenue. It cost $176,543 and was built to cover the rapidly expanding east side and Eastland Shopping Center. Most of the stations built during this period were similar, but 23's is the only one of its kind. It is similar to the others but built with a huge sloping roof to blend in with the neighborhood.

In anticipation of opening this station, a second engine had been placed in service at Station 20 (Engine 20A) in 1958. When 23's was completed this engine and crew were moved in with a years' worth of runs and experience in this area of town. In 1970 Ladder 21 was moved to 23's to give better coverage of the east side.

LOYALTY

The station responds on mutual aid with Whitehall, Mifflin Township (Gahanna), Truro Township (Reynoldsburg) and Madison Township (Canal Winchester). It also responds to Port Columbus International Airport.

The station currently has an engine, ladder and medic.

HAMILTON ROAD & E. LIVINGSTON AVENUE

Station Twentyfour

Station 24 is currently one of the busiest stations in Columbus. It was built in 1960 at a cost of $197,265. It is located at 1585 Morse Road at the intersection of Karl Road, one of the busiest intersections in the city. A portion of the original parcel of land was sold to a commercial establishment for $100,00 and the money was used to purchase two new pieces of apparatus for the department. The station is a one-story brick station with centrally located bays and living quarters on the sides

For the first few years the area was primarily residential. Then several shopping centers, motels and numerous apartment complexes grew up around the major shopping center called Northland Mall. It is one of the most densely populated areas of Columbus, second only to the University Area. Station 24 also responds into Westerville, Worthington, Clinton Township and Gahanna.

Station 24 Dragonslayers

MERCY

1585 Morse Road

Station Twentyfive

First to Strike

Station 25 was the "Airport" station at Port Columbus International Airport. The airport's first fire protection was provided by the U.S. Navy, which operated out of military style buildings located at 651 N. Hamilton Road.

In 1959, in preparation for the Navy ceasing operations at the airport, Columbus firefighters moved into the engine house to be trained on the crash equipment. The three military crash trucks would be left on loan until the airport could purchase new trucks.

In 1960, plans were made to build a new engine house. The future station would be located on airport property and be owned by the airport. The new location would provide immediate access to the main runway and the terminal area.

On July 25, 1966, Station 25 was opened at 4925 Sawyer Drive. Fire equipment responded both on and off of the airport and was available to other fire departments by special request.

The station was a one-story brick building with eight apparatus bays, four bays on each end of the central living quarters.

In 1995, after 36 years of Columbus firefighters protecting Columbus air travelers, the airport bid out crash/rescue services to a private company. The fire station was turned over to the new service and Station 25 ceased to exist. All Columbus personnel and equipment were removed and distributed throughout the division.

Later that same year, on July 1, 1995, Station 25 was reborn at 739 West Third Avenue (old 9's) when the Medical Training Center (MTC) was moved to the new fire administration complex on Parsons Avenue.

Built in 1961, the station is located in the Ohio State University area, adjacent to the City of Grandview. Engine 25, Medic 25 and a boat respond to the University area, the nearby Olentangy River, and the many shopping and commercial complexes in the area. There is heavy student housing nearby, including numerous high-rise dorms. The campus, numerous sports complexes and many research facilities also dot the area. The station runs mutual aid with Grandview and Upper Arlington.

739 W. THIRD AVENUE

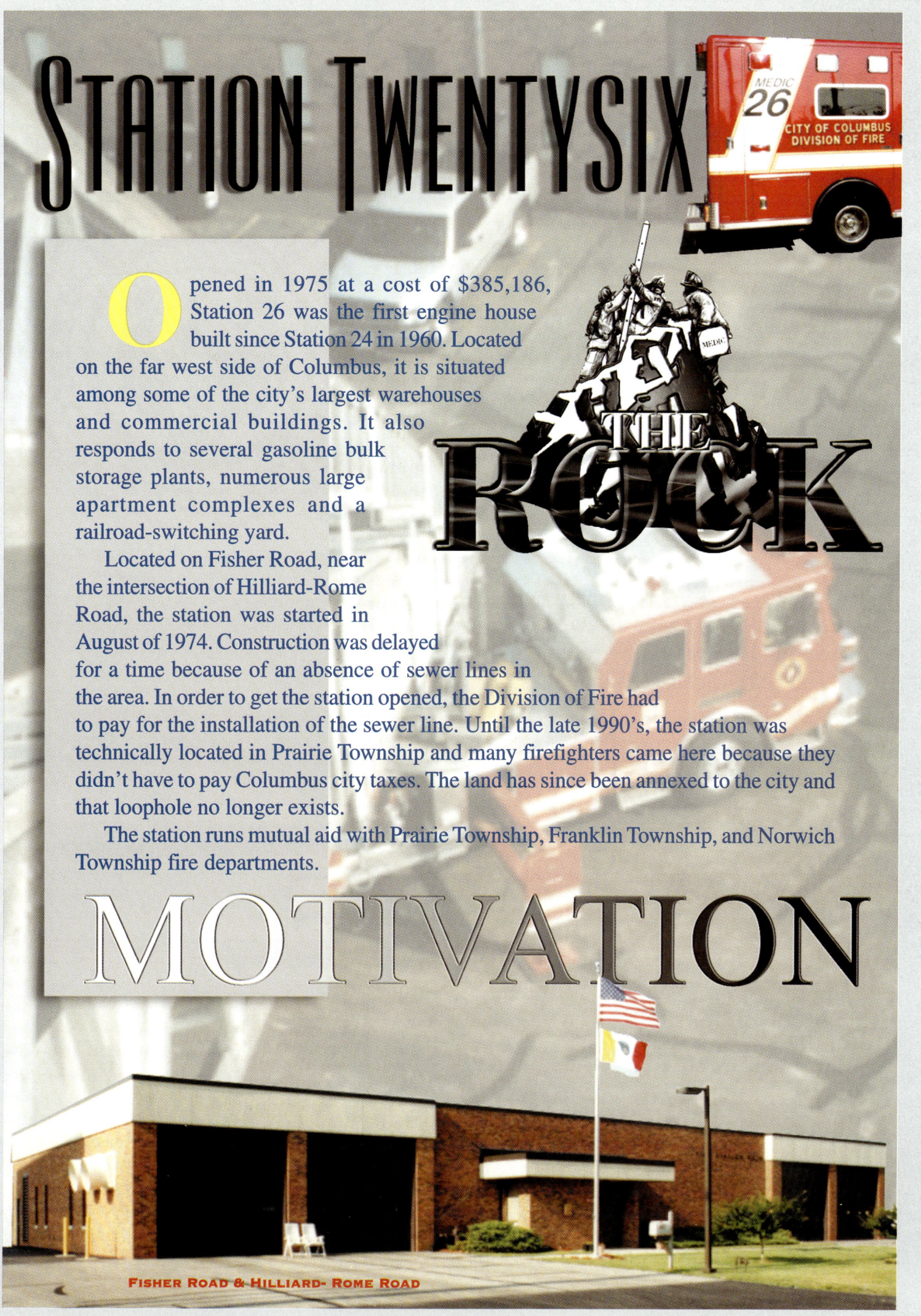

Station Twentysix

Opened in 1975 at a cost of $385,186, Station 26 was the first engine house built since Station 24 in 1960. Located on the far west side of Columbus, it is situated among some of the city's largest warehouses and commercial buildings. It also responds to several gasoline bulk storage plants, numerous large apartment complexes and a railroad-switching yard.

Located on Fisher Road, near the intersection of Hilliard-Rome Road, the station was started in August of 1974. Construction was delayed for a time because of an absence of sewer lines in the area. In order to get the station opened, the Division of Fire had to pay for the installation of the sewer line. Until the late 1990's, the station was technically located in Prairie Township and many firefighters came here because they didn't have to pay Columbus city taxes. The land has since been annexed to the city and that loophole no longer exists.

The station runs mutual aid with Prairie Township, Franklin Township, and Norwich Township fire departments.

THE ROCK

MOTIVATION

FISHER ROAD & HILLIARD- ROME ROAD

Station Twentyseven

Station 27 was built in 1978 and is located at 7560 Smokey Row Road, at Billingsley Road. It cost $420,000 to build and is located on a parcel of land that also includes two large water towers. The building is one-story brick with centrally located living quarters, two bays on each side of the station and no basement. Because of its "outpost" location, the station is known as "The Great Northwest".

Engine, Ladder and Medic 27 respond to largely residential areas and numerous shopping centers. They also respond to the outerbelt located next to the station, but must enter I-270 from Sawmill Road, since there are no ramps on Smokey Row Road.

They also respond with mutual aid to Washington Township and the City of Worthington.

PRIDE

CITY OF COLUMBUS
THE GREAT NORTHWEST

129

Station Twentyeight

Station 28 is located at 3240 McCutcheon Road, at the intersection of Stelzer Road and McCutcheon Road. It was dedicated October 4, 1981, and cost $720,000. It is a one-story brick station with living quarters in the center and four bays, two on each end. It is located in the northeast portion of the city and has a variety of response areas. It responds to Port Columbus Airport and numerous residential and apartment communities. It also responds to the large Limited clothing warehouse complex and the new Easton Shopping area.

The station is equipped with an engine, ladder and medic. Mutual aid to the area includes Mifflin Township and Clinton Township fire departments.

PROFESSIONAL

3240 McCutcheon Road

Station Twentynine

Station 29 is located in the Little Turtle condominium complex in the northeast part of Columbus. Groundbreaking occurred July 22, 1983 and when completed, the station cost $714,000. Residents of the area had petitioned for a firehouse for several years after a series of fires destroyed several of the wood sided and wood shingled roof buildings. Availability of an affordable and suitable parcel of land was a major problem. After several years of planning and negotiating, the developer donated a 1.3 acre parcel of land at the entrance to the Little Turtle complex. The donated parcel saved the city $75,000 and provided an efficient location to serve the area.

Addressed at 5151 Little Turtle Way, at the intersection of Dublin-Granville Road, fire protection is just minutes away from the large residential complex. The building is a one-story, 10,500 square foot building with living quarters in the center, and two bays on each end.

RELIABLE

5151 LITTLE TURTLE WAY

Station Thirty

THE RESORT

Station 30 is located in a large shopping complex called Mill Run. The address is 3555 Fishinger Boulevard and is near the intersection of Fishinger Road and Dublin Road. The station opened August 1, 1988 at a cost of $850,000. The land was donated by the complex developer with a stipulation that the station blend in with adjoining buildings, and the landscaping be kept on a par with the surrounding properties.

This station is the first Columbus firehouse built to accommodate female firefighters, with individual bedrooms and restrooms. Stations 30, and Station 31 at Bolton Field Airport, were built from the same plans and at the same time, saving time and money. Lack of storage space and a basement was a particular problem when exercise equipment was installed in all Columbus fire stations; in 30's and 31's it had to be installed in the "living room". This was corrected in stations built after 1988.

Due to the expanding growth of Columbus in the northwest area, an agreement was made with Norwich Township Fire Department for an engine to run out of the Norwich Township station located on the Franklin County fairgrounds. Engine 30 ran into Columbus areas from this station from 1986 until the opening of Station 30 in 1988. Although Norwich and Columbus had no automatic mutual aid agreement, the crews "unofficially" backed each other up when needed. The two stations still enjoy an exceptional relationship and both departments now have automatic response with each other.

Station 30 is also "just across the river" from Upper Arlington and had a similar experience with Upper Arlington's Station 71. When Station 71 was being remodeled, Medic 71 moved into and responded from Station 30 for several months.

In addition to mutual aid with Norwich Township and Upper Arlington, Station 30 also responds with Washington Township Fire Department.

The station is an all brick, one story station with living quarters in the center and two bays on each end. Station 30 covers Griggs Dam Park, located on the Scioto River just east of the station. The station is surrounded by a shopping complex, several churches, numerous residential and apartment complexes, and a wide variety of restaurants.

RESOLVE

Station Thirtyone
Wild-Wild West

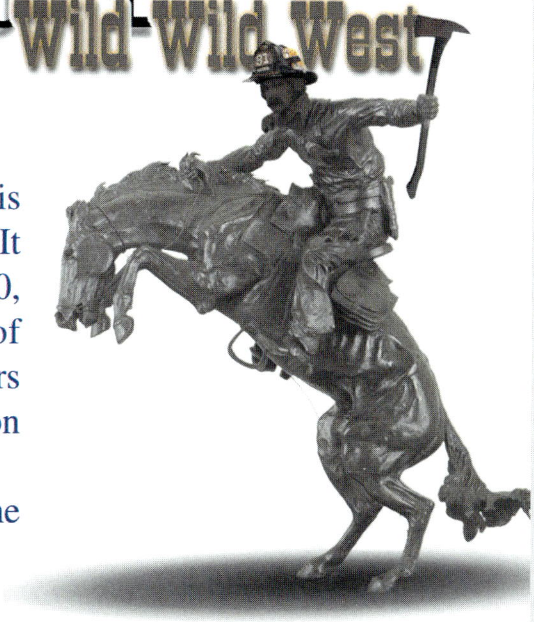

Station 31 is located at 5305 Alkire Road, but is known as the Bolton Field Airport fire station. It was built in 1988 at the same time as Station 30, costing $850,000. The land was owned by the City of Columbus as part of the Bolton Airport. The station covers the southwest portion of the city, and is just east of Norton Road.

It is a one-story brick station with living quarters in the center and four apparatus bays. It was built on the same plans as Station 30 to save time and money. It was the second station built to be "unisex", with individual bedrooms and bathrooms.

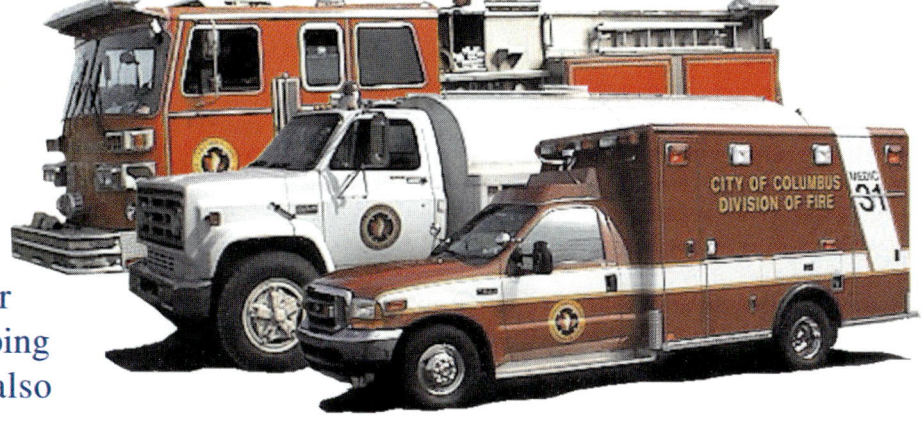

Their response area includes the airport, large warehouses and trucking companies, numerous car dealerships and a large shopping center complex. There are also large residential and apartment complexes in the area.

SERVICE

5305 ALKIRE ROAD

Station Thirtytwo

Station 32 is currently the most easterly station in Columbus. It is located at 3675 Gender Road. It cost $1.1 million and was opened December 11, 1991. It is a one-story brick station with two bays on each end of the central living quarters. It was built on the same plans as Station 11 and the two were built at the same time to save money.

The third and fourth stations designed to include women, 32's and 11's were improved over 30's and 31's by adding basements and increasing the size of the kitchen and living areas. The stations now have about 4900 square feet of living space.

Station 32 covers a large shopping complex area, including a Penney's Distribution Center, residential areas and the nearby Inter-state I-70 and I-270 outer belt.

THE BEAST OF THE EAST

ENGINE LADDER 32 MEDIC

VALOR

3675 GENDER ROAD

134

Station Thirtythree

The Great White North

Station 33, the "Polaris" station, was opened on April 24, 1994. It is located at 440 Lazelle Road and the cost to build was $1,241,000. The station is located at the current northern edge of Columbus, and it was the first station to have a "paramedic" engine. This provided a trained paramedic as part of the crew and all of the associated ACLS equipment that an EMS vehicle would carry. The purpose was to provide faster EMS response to this outer area of the city, including the Polaris Amphitheater complex that would typically have large numbers of people during scheduled events. Under a major restructuring of the EMS system, every engine house in the city would eventually have a "paramedic" engine and a paramedic vehicle.

When new in 1994, Engine 33 cost $400,000 and Ladder 33's aerial platform cost $700,000. The running district includes the rapidly expanding Polaris shopping, commercial and residential areas. Mutual aid responses include the cities of Westerville and Worthington.

The station is one-story with two bays on each end of the centrally located living quarters.

VIGILENCE

440 LAZELLE ROAD

LADDER 33

Future Stations

Station 34

Station 34 was planned to be located on Wilcox Road, south of Tuttle Crossing. The station will be similar to Station 17 located on West Broad Street. It will be a one-story brick building, with two bays on each end of the central living quarters. This station will be located in the northwest area of the city, bordered by areas of Norwich Township, and Washington Township.

The response area will include a major shopping complex surrounded by numerous restaurants and smaller retail malls. Major office complexes dot the area and more are being planned. The station should be completed in 2003 or 2004.

Stations 35 and 36

Stations planned for the future include a station on the far east side and far south side. Station 35, planned for the far east side, will be near Waggoner and Wengert Roads, north of East Broad Street. Station 36 will be located south near London-Groveport Road and Shook Road. This is west of the entrance to the Rickenbacker Airport and Industrial Complex. Both of these stations will be one-story stations similar to Station 17 on West Broad Street.

Columbus Division of Fire Officers

Chief

Pettus, Ned, Sr.
Fire Chief
01-24-77

Assistant Chiefs

Braun, Richard A.
Executive Asst. Chief
10-01-73

Cox, Warren R.
Emer. Ser. Bur. 1U
10-14-75

Ellis, Karry L.
Emer. Ser. Bur. 2U
04-07-80

Keefer, Joseph E.
Emer. Ser. Bur. 1U
12-15-63

Lawhorn, Carl C.
Training Bur.
02-17-69

Rees, John E.
Supp. Ser. Bur.
10-15-72
Retired 8-18-01

Vincent, Daniel J.
Fire Pre. Bur.
Retired 1-6-01

Deputy Chiefs

Bardocz, Charles H.
Batt 3 3U
10-17-77

Mason, Jerry L.
Emer. Ser. Bur. 2U
10-14-75

Paxton, Gregory A.
Emer. Ser. Bur. 3U
03-16-81

Battalion Chiefs

Arnold, Yolanda J.
Floating Officer 3U
03-28-83

Babb, Robert O.
Train Bur.
10-14-75

Bauman, Craig D.
Batt 1 2U
12-11-78

Beverly, Thomas
Batt 7 1U
10-17-77

Bishop, William L.
EMS-11 3U
11-29-87

Butcher, Ronald L.
Batt 5 1U
07-29-85

Coles, Robert W.
Fire Pre. Bur.
10-14-75

Davis, Kenneth W.
Batt 2 1U
10-14-75
Retired 7-21-01

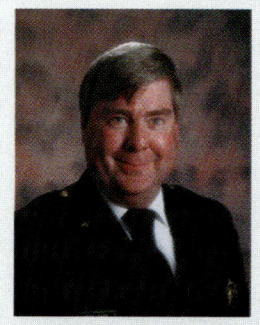

Devine, Mark R.
Batt 3 2U
12-26-72

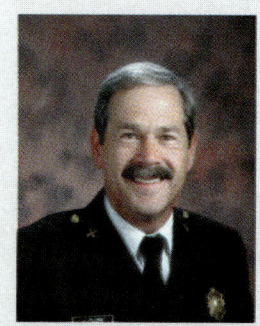

Flynn, James M.
Batt 3 1U
10-15-72

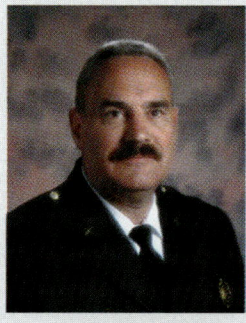

Foote, Herbert M.
Safety Officer
10-17-77

Fultz, Michael
Bur. of Admin.
04-03-78

Gaal, Richard A.
Batt 4 2U
02-04-85

Gillenwater, Dennis R.
Supp. Ser. Bur.
01-24-77

Griffith, Johnny C.
Batt 2 3U
10-17-77

Hackett, Tommy E.
Batt 5 2U
03-12-73

Jackson, Robert D.
Batt 6 1U
10-01-73

Johnson, James M.
Batt 4 3U
12-11-78

Moore, Sean P.
Batt 7 2U
07-13-87

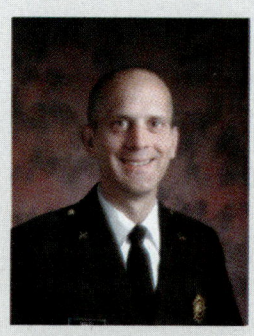

Mosley, Craig C.
Floating Officer 2U
10-29-79

139

Battalion Chiefs

O'Connor, Kevin M.
Batt 3 3U
04-03-89

Petersen, Paul. J.
Batt 7 2U
01-20-69
Retired

Schmidt, Robert L.
Batt 1 1U
01-02-71

Smith, Douglas J.
Batt 4 3U
04-12-82

Spaeth, Randy W.
Batt 2 1U
10-17-77

Trojack, Terrance A.
Batt 6 3U
01-24-77

Vedra, William F.
Fire Alarm Off.
04-12-82

Walton, David J.
Float. Off. Batt. 4 3U
02-04-85

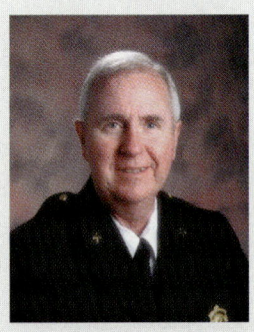

White, Howard E.
Batt 1 3U
10-15-72
Retired 10-27-01

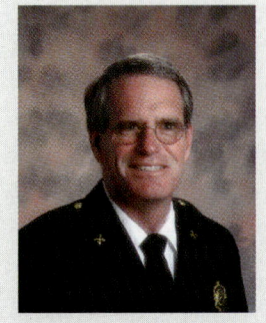

Wintering, James M.
Batt 7 3U
10-29-79

CAPTAINS

Alexander, James H.
E-21 3U
12-11-78

Arruda, David P.
E-21 3U
04-12-82

Atwood, Stewart B.
Pro. Standards Unit
02-04-85

Ballard, Richard D.
Float. Off. Batt. 1U
07-13-87

Barrett, Patrick M.
L-12 3U
10-29-79

Barton, Laurence G.
Research/Development
07-30-72

Basil, Steven R.
Division Liason
10-17-77

Beard, Robert
Retired 3-17-01

Belcher, Douglas S.
E-8 2U
04-03-89

Biancone, Richard L.
L-24 3U
07-13-87

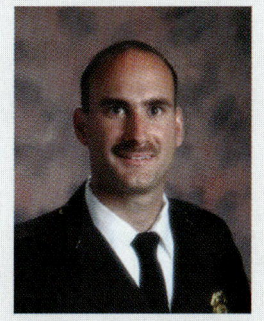

Birkhimer, Gerald C.
EMS-13 3U
07-29-85

Boham, Richard R.
E-2 2U
10-31-77

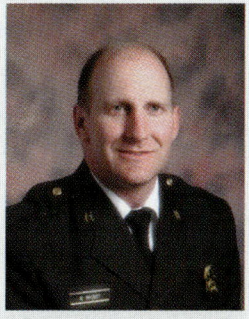

Brobst, William E. Jr.
E-4 1U
07-29-85

Campbell, Charles E.
EMS-11 1U
10-14-75

Cannell, James R. Jr.
L-33 1U
12-11-89

Casto, Ronald A.
E-14 1U
10-15-72

Cordle, Terrence J.
EMS-11 2U
01-02-71

Dennis, James P.
E-25 2U
12-11-78

Farrand, David V.
L-22 3U
07-29-85

Forst, James G.
Safety Officer 1U
03-16-81

141

CAPTAINS

Fowler, Michael A.
L-8 1U
12-11-78

Francisco, Lawrence W.
Float. Off. Batt. 1 2U
01-26-87

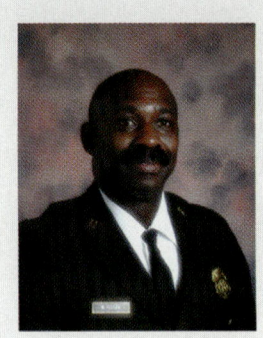

Fullen, Wesley H.
Fire Pre. Bur.
02-04-85

Geist, John E.
Supp. Ser. Bur.
01-02-71
Retired

Goss, Jerry L.
Executive Office
12-24-73

Gross, Earl B.
L-2 3U
06-06-71

Hayworth, Roby S.
Train. Bur.
09-16-68

Heselden, Steven B.
E-11 2U
04-12-82

Kauble, William C.
Safety Officer 2U
10-01-73

Kennedy, David J.
E-17 2U
10-29-79

Kravig, Russell G.
E-31 2U
12-11-78
Retired

Lash, Gregory W.
L-1 2U
03-12-73

Lawless, Mark
E-16 2U
03-16-81

Lewis, Arthur A.
U/A E-21 2U
07-29-85

Lewis, James T.
Train. Bur.
01-26-87

Liddle, Joseph H.
F007/3
03-16-81

Mangini, Steven P.
E-19 2U
10-15-72

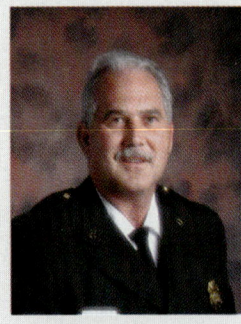

McCoy, Lewis
Safety Officer 3U
11-12-73

Moloney, Patrick J.
E-6 1U
02-04-85

Moore, Larry A.
E-20 2U
03-16-81

142

CAPTAINS

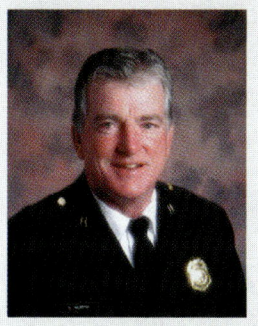

Murphy, Richard F.
L-32 3U
03-12-73

Olney, David F.
L-23 1U
02-04-85

Penwell, Charles A.
L-10 1U
03-28-83

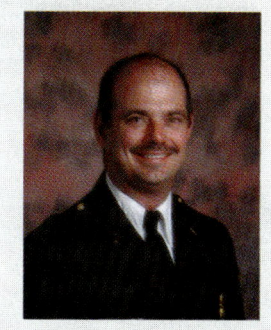

Price, Robert L.
E-15 1U
02-04-85

Reardon, Kevin S.
L-28 1U
03-16-81

Robinson, Robert K.
Supp. Ser. Bur. 40hrs
05-19-96

Roggenkamp, David L.
E-7 2U
02-03-86

Ross, Douglas B.
E-7 1U
07-29-85

Saltsman, Stephen V.
Fire Pre. Bur.
07-13-87

Searle, Kent C.
E-4 1U
03-28-83

Stephens, Michael D.
E-29 2U
10-01-73

Strahan, Scott E.
E-23 2U
08-20-91

Tippett, James
L-10 1U
Retired 6-10-00

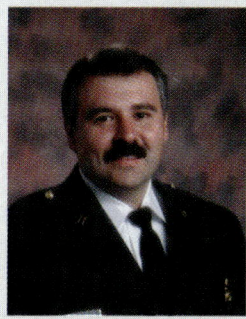

Vingle, John M.
L-13 3U
11-30-87

Whiting, David K.
L-15 2U
07-13-87

Wilt, John C.
Train. Bur.
02-04-85

Wood, Johnnie E.
L-26 1U
10-17-77

LIEUTENANTS

Arnold, Eddie R.
E-20 3U
03-28-83

Barton, Russell O.
EMS-16 1U
04-07-80

Battle, Gregory L.
U/A Batt. 1 3U
08-20-91

Billingham, Donna J.
E-1 2U
01-26-87

Blair, Christopher A.
E-4 2U
03-03-91

Blizzard, James
EMS-15 2U
Retired 1-20-01

Bonaventura, Pat M.
EMS-16 2U
09-07-69

Borgan, Garey W.
E-23 3U
11-30-87

Brunney, Philip D. Jr.
E-17 1U
07-13-87

Brunney, Philip D. Sr.
E-32 1U
12-26-72

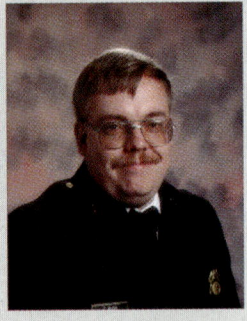

Bush, Terry K.
E-19 3U
02-03-86

Callahan, Richard D. Jr.
U/A Batt. 4 2U
03-03-91

Caserta, Matthew R.
L-15 3U
04-03-89

Catt, Brian C.
E-25 3U
07-25-88

Chapman, Steven
E-33 2U
10-29-79

Christ, Thomas
Retired 6-23-01

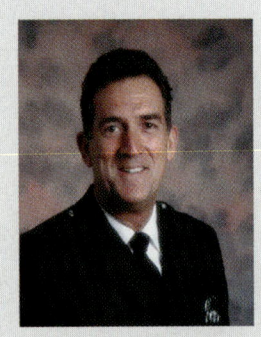

Clemons, Steven C.
Pro. Standards Unit
10-17-77

Cloud, Robert
Retired 1-20-01

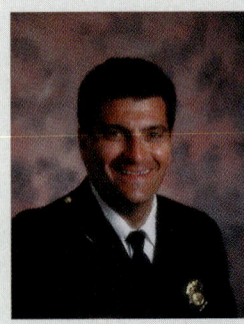

Conti, Richard A.
E-13 2U
04-12-82

144

LIEUTENANTS

Cook, David R.
L-12 1U
10-15-72

Cordle, Timothy D.
E-15 2U
12-26-72

Cosmar, Rickard D.
EMS-12 3U
07-25-88

Cox, John H.
Retired 11-25-00

Crites, Jared D.
E-18 3U
03-03-91

D'Andrea, Joseph
E-11 3U
03-16-81

Dadum, Robert
Retired 1-20-01

Davis, David S.
L-1 1U
04-12-82

Davis, James E.
Float. Off. Batt. 1 1U
11-28-88

Davis, Woodrow X.
E-15 3U
12-11-78

Decarlo, Frank
E-29 3U
10-01-73

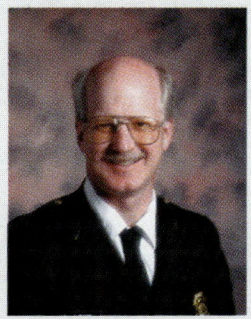

Delong, Thomas F.
EMS-13 1U
07-29-85

Dickson, Charles R.
E-28 3U
04-07-80

Dipietro, Gary
Retired 6-25-00

Duckworth, Terry J.
L-1 3U
04-12-82

Dunning, Robert E.
E-19 1U
05-03-70

Durham, Lynn A.
EMS-17 2U
03-28-83

Eplin, Donald P.
E-21 1U
04-03-89

Erb, Timothy H.
U/A Batt. 3 3U
03-03-91

145

LIEUTENANTS

Evergin, Judy A.
EMS-14 3U
03-28-83

Fiasconi, Michael A.
E-7 3U
04-03-78

Fulcher, George A. III
U/A Batt. 1 2U
04-12-82

Funk, Shawn D.
Float. Off. Batt. 1 1U
08-07-89

Green, Marcus A.
L-24 2U
04-12-82

Guay, Roland C. III
L-10 2U
03-16-81

Haley, David S.
E-2 3U
03-28-88

Happ, Jeffrey M.
E-7 2U
06-14-93

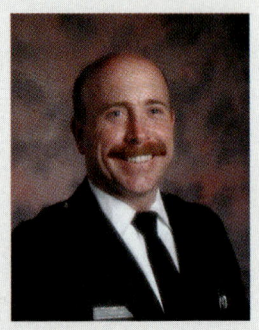

Harrow, Larry J.
Float. Off. Batt. 2 2U
07-29-85

Harvey, Dan
L-10 2U
Retired 6-10-00

Hayes, Richard A.
EMS-16 3U
03-16-81

Head, Thomas M.
FAO 2U
10-17-77

Hennosy, David J.
U/A Batt. 3 1U
11-30-87

Heughebart, Stephen Jr.
U/A Batt. 3 1U
03-28-88

Hilbert, Larry L.
E-23 1U
10-01-73

Hill, John M.
L-13 2U
12-26-72
Retired

Hinton, Larry C.
E-22 2U
10-15-72

Howard, Gregory M.
E-14 2U
03-28-88

Hunley, Paul B.
L-28 2U
08-07-89

Igo, James S.
L-27 1U
12-24-73

146

LIEUTENANTS

Jahn, Jeffery A. EMS-12 2U 11-30-87	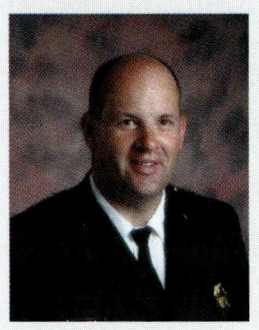 Kable, David B. E-13 3U 07-13-87	 Kitchen, Michael D. E-1 3U 10-01-73	 Knapp, Gary L. L-23 3U 04-07-80	 Krummel, Scott D. EMS-15 2U 02-03-86
 Kruse, Clay E-28 2U 11-28-88	 Legg, Charles W. Jr. E-28 1U 04-07-80	 Leis, Steven R. E-10 2U 01-26-87	 Lieb, Martin E. E-27 2U 03-28-83	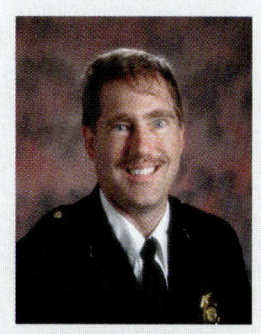 Lieb, Michael J. E-6 3U 10-29-79
 Litteral, Jeffrey L. E-22 1U 10-17-77	 Loschiavo, Salvatore Jr. L-32 1U 12-26-72	 Marsh, Terry L. E-21 2U 01-26-87	 Martin, Steven C. E-3 1U 11-30-87	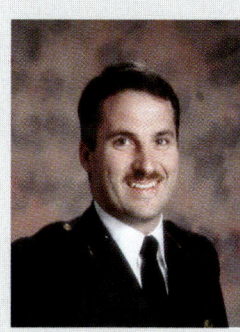 Mason, Raymond A. L-23 2U 07-13-87
 Maxwell, Robert R. L-22 1U 07-26-64	 McCann, C. Dennis Jr.	 McConaha, James E. L-8 2U 12-11-78	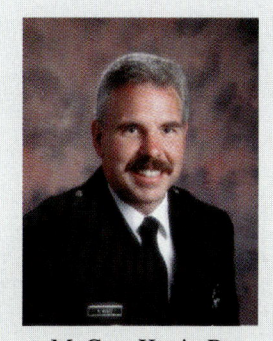 McGee, Kevin R. Float. Off. Batt. 3 1U 01-26-87	 McKeen, Michael W. Float. Off. Batt. 5 3U 08-07-89

LIEUTENANTS

McKimmins, Kevin
U/A Batt. 1 3U
03-03-91

McKnight, Michael S.
E-2 2U
01-26-87

McLeod, Frederick C.
U/A Batt. 5 1U
02-04-85

McMurray, Mark L.
Float. Off. Batt. 2 2U
02-03-86

McVay, James A.
EMS-14 2U
02-03-86

Mileff, Richard S.
L-2 2U
08-07-89

Miller, Don L.
L-22 2U
10-14-75

Mitchell, James H.
E-27 3U
08-07-89

Moore, Francis R.
E-30 1U
03-12-73

Moore, Timothy D.
EMS-14 1U
12-11-89

Motter, William E. Jr.
Float. Off. Batt. 4 2U
07-13-87

Murdock, Arnold C.
E-12 1U
02-04-85

Murphy, Michael C.
E-9 3U
10-15-72

Nance, Bernard A.
Train. Bur.
10-01-73
Retired

Neal, Terry L.
Fire Pre. Bur.
02-04-85

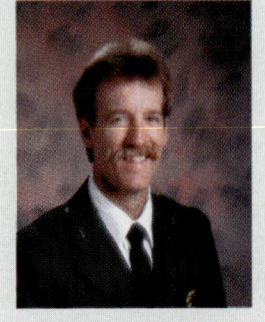

Nightingale, Stephen P.
E-9 1U
04-03-89

O'Connor, James M.
Float. Off. Batt. 1 3U
12-11-89

Oldaker, Kenneth D.II
E-32 3U
01-26-87

O'Rourke, Kevin M.
E-10 1U
03-28-83

148

LIEUTENANTS

Pearson, James C.
E-11 1U
02-04-85

Phillips, Marquis D.
Float. Off. Batt. 5 2U
08-20-91

Polaski, Don M.
E-16 3U
12-26-72

Preece, William S.
E-31 1U
10-31-71

Prince, Joseph R.
E-5 1U
10-29-79

Quick, Timothy M.
Fire Pre. Bur.
12-11-89

Reall, Jack E.
E-13 1U
12-11-89

Reeves, Michael R.
L-27 2U
10-14-75

Reid, Edward D.
E-27 1U
04-07-80

Rich, William C.
E-5 2U
10-29-79

Richard, Joseph C.
Fire Pre. Bur.
07-29-85

Richardson, Richard D.
E-24 2U
07-25-88

Rodenbeck, Douglas H.
E-29 1U
10-14-75

Rohr, John D.
E-2 1U
01-26-87

Ross, William G.
E-3 2U
07-13-87

Ruddle, Michael A.
E-2 1U
03-03-91

Rudman, Bruce A.
Bur. of Admin.
07-29-85

Sachs, Michael E.
E-9 2U
01-26-87

Sauer, Timothy M.
E-33 3U
08-04-68

149

LIEUTENANTS

Sawyer, David B.
E-24 1U
04-07-80

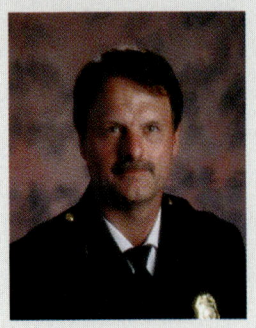

Schoch, Rick S.
EMS-13 2U
03-28-83

Schrader, Daniel J.
EMS-15 1U
10-17-77

Schroeder, John E.
E-12 2U
03-28-83

Scott, John E. II
E-31 3U
02-04-85

Scott, Terry L.
EMS-17 1U
10-14-75

Simkins, John W.
E-24 3U
02-19-67

Simpson, Steven E.
L-2 1U
01-26-87

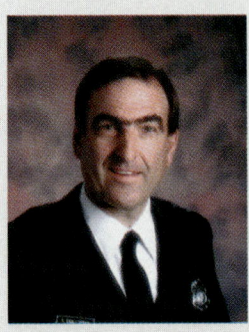

Smallsreed, Stephen W.
U/A Batt. 6 2U
02-04-85

Smith, Jeffrey E.
U/A Batt. 1 3U
07-29-85

Smith, Rodney K.
L-15 1U
10-29-79

Smith, William G.
Fire Pre. Bur.
04-12-82

Sowers, Robert E.
L-26 2U
03-03-91

Sowers, Robert E. Sr.
L-12 2U
11-12-73

Stevens, Lawrence
Fire Pre. Bur.
02-04-85

LIEUTENANTS

Stewart, Leroy
Float. Off. Batt. 7 1U
12-11-78

Stone, Carl B.
L-26 3U
02-22-70

Strominger, Timothy J.
U/A Batt. 2 3U
10-29-79

Sullivan, John E.
E-14 3U
06-06-71

Swanson, Edgar
Retired 8-5-00

Tanner, William J.
FAO 3U
04-03-78

Torrie, John C.
E-3 3U
07-29-85

Trucco, Michael R.
L-8 3U
10-17-77

Vedra, Michael J.
E-30 2U
07-13-87

Walker, Gerald
Retired 1-20-01

LIEUTENANTS

Wallace, George H. EMS-15 3U 03-03-91	Waters, Terry D. E-32 2U 12-11-78	Weber, Danny L. E-16 1U 10-29-79	Weldon, Donald L. E-26 2U 02-03-86	Werner, Tom E. E-18 2U 04-03-78
White, Dwayne G. U/A Batt. 6 1U 07-13-87	Wiley, Arthur W. Fire Alarm Office 10-17-77	Wiley, Clifford E. L-28 3U 12-11-78	Williams, Bryan M. E-20 1U 03-28-88	Williamson, Clyde D. E-10 3U 01-26-87
Williamson, Jeffrey F. L-10 3U 01-02-71	Williamson, Monte L. Float. Off. Batt. 6 3U 10-29-79	Willison, William S. E-17 3U 02-04-85	Wine, Ray E-26 3U 03-28-83	Witosky, David C. E-8 3U 11-30-87
Wollett, Lawrence R. Jr. Float. Off. Batt. 3 3U 07-29-85	Young, John R. E-6 2U 10-14-75	Young, Paul T. L-13 1U 10-29-79	Zuber, Michael J. EMS-12 1U 08-07-89	Zwilling, Donald G. E-22 3U 03-28-83

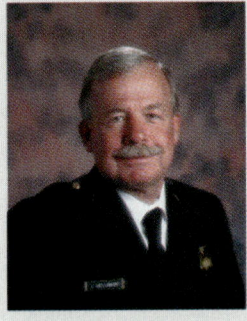

Columbus Division of Fire Firefighters

ADAMS • ATWOOD   FIREFIGHTERS

Adams, Michael R.
E-28 2U
10-29-79

Aldridge, Jeffery D.
L-13 3U
04-03-89

Alexander, Robert H.
Fire Pre. Bur.
04-03-78

Allen, David T.
U/A Batt 3 1U
10-26-98

Allen, Gregory D.
E-12 2U
01-28-96

Allen, Patrick M.
U/A Batt 5 3U
05-16-99

Allison, Deborah S.
E-1 1U
05-04-97

Almon, Billy R.
Fire Pre. Bur.
02-03-86

Alston, Michael R.
L-26 2U
02-04-85

Alvarado, Phillip W.
L-33 1U
11-28-88

Alwood, Julia E.
FAO 2U
07-25-88

Amick, James E.
Sta. 11 40hr.
05-19-96

Anderson, Allan L.
E-4 3U
05-17-98

Anderson, Roger L.
E-14 1U
08-20-91

Ansel, John J.
Emer. Services
12-11-78

Arehart, William B. Jr.
E-1 3U
12-11-89

Armstrong, Ballard M.
E-20 2U
09-11-94

Arnett, Jeffrey
L-32 1U
07-26-92

Arruda, Robin A.
E-24 1U
12-11-89

Arthur, Ryan
E-23 1U
12-18-96

Ashley, Meaka D. Jr.
Background 40hrs.
02-03-86

Atkinson, Robert M.
L-28 3U
01-28-96

Atwood, Arn
E-2 2U
12-11-89

Atwood, Norman P.
Train. Bur.
05-17-98

154

Atwood, Steven L.
L-27 1U
04-12-82

Avery, Robert
E-16 2U
03-13-94

Ayers, Matt S.
E-13 3U
12-14-97

Ayers, Steven
Retired 6-23-01

Ayers, Steven D.
L-22 3U
12-11-89

Bahl, Kevin R.
E-30 3U
04-09-95

Bailey, Alan G.
Background 40hrs.
04-12-82

Bailey, Christopher A.
E-29 1U
09-11-94

Bailey, Matthew L.
E-14 3U
01-28-96

Bair, Chad R.
E-10 3U
12-15-96

Baker, Scott E.
E-2 1U
03-03-91

Bakle, Richard J.
E-24 3U
10-31-99

Ballard, John D. Jr.
E-32 2U
12-14-97

Barber, William F.
E-4 1U
07-25-88

Barcus, Robert
Retired 1-11-01

Barlow, Donald C.
E-14 2U
03-28-83

Barnett, Jeffrey
E-33 3U
05-16-99

Barnhart, Dale E.
E-5 1U
09-11-94

Barrett, John A.
E-2 2U
03-28-88

Barrick, Brian C.
L-23 2U
05-17-98

Barth, Kevin L.
E-7 1U
04-09-95

Barton, Timothy D.
E-1 3U
05-17-98

Bash, Todd W.
E-32 3U
10-31-99

Basham, Jeffery R.
L-2 3U
01-28-96

FIREFIGHTERS

ATWOOD • BASHAM

155

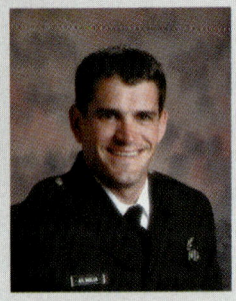

Basler • Bernard

Firefighters

Basler, Glen K. E-26 3U 10-26-98	 Bates, Michael J. E-14 3U 03-16-81	 Bauer, Gregory L. E-21 3U 01-28-96	 Bauer, Joe M. E-14 3U 01-28-96	 Baugh, David R.• E-10 3U 01-28-96	 Beale, Charles L. Jr. E-29 3U 03-28-83
 Beatty, Mark A. E-30 1U 07-29-85	 Beaty, James R. II E-10 1U 12-15-96	 Beavers, Kenyon E. Fire Pre. Bur. 11-30-87	 Bebout, Darrell J. L-23 2U 04-12-82	 Bebout, Harry E. L-2 2U 04-03-89	 Beckett, Matthew L. E-25 1U 04-09-95
 Beckley, Russell A. E-5 2U 04-03-78	 Beckman, Michael W. Sta. 6 40hr. 10-15-72	 Bednarski, Brian H. E-19 2U 10-26-98	 Beery, Todd M. E-13 1U 06-14-93	 Begley, James R. E-22 3U 09-10-95	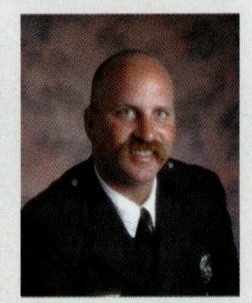 Behrens, Douglas A. L-1 2U 03-28-88
 Belcher, Brian K. E-2 2U 06-14-93	 Belcher, Gregory R-4 2U 11-28-88	 Belcher, Stephen W. E-3 3U 04-09-95	 Bellisari, Tony A. E-10 3U 06-14-93	 Belt, Richard C. L-23 1U 05-17-98	 Bendure, Jason M. U/A Batt 1 2U 10-26-98
 Bendure, Stephen W. E-25 2U 10-01-73	 Benjamin, Scott D. E-28 3U 12-15-96	 Bennison, Stephen W. E-18 3U 04-09-95	 Bergin, Steven M. E-24 1U 08-07-89	 Bergman, John P. FAO 1U 02-03-86	 Bernard, John P. E-31 3U 12-14-97

Bernzweig, David T. E-7 2U 12-15-96	Best, Michael D. E-7 1U 08-20-91	 Bevilacoua, Mark L-24 1U 11-30-87	Biddlestone, Glen R. FAO 2U 04-03-89	Biedenharn, Michael E-10 3U 03-03-91	Biggs, Philip M. E-16 2U 05-04-97
 Bigham, Nathan A. L-8 1U 07-27-92	 Bigham, Richard L. L-8 1U 07-13-87	 Blackburn, Scott A. E-28 2U 05-16-99	 Blackwell, Michael S. L-12 3U 11-28-88	 Blair, David B. R-16 2U 03-03-91	 Blair, Jeffrey S. E-24 3U 09-11-94
 Blevins, Matthew R. E-23 3U 05-19-96	 Bobo, Thomas H. R-11 1U 04-07-80	 Bocook, Edwin J. L-26 1U 03-03-91	 Boehm, Robert K. L-33 2U 03-03-91	 Boerner, Richard E-30 2U 01-26-87	 Bohanan, Gerald S. E-3 2U 05-19-96
 Bollon, Richard V. Train. Bur 10-17-71	 Borghese, Frank S. L-24 3U 06-14-93	 Boso, Christopher A. E-4 3U 09-10-95	 Botkins, Ronald A. E-6 2U 07-27-92	 Bova, Philip C. R-11 1U 03-13-94	 Bowen, Garnet L. Jr. E-31 3U 11-28-88
 Bower, Paul R. E-7 1U 09-10-95	 Bowersock, Jeffrey S. R-17 3U 03-13-94	 Boyce, Dayle Fire Pre. Bur. 02-04-85	 Boyd, Kevin T. L-1 2U 03-28-88	 Boyer, Terry R. E-6 2U 08-20-91	 Brady, Larry K. E-30 3U 03-13-94

Breckenridge • Cagle

Firefighters

Breckenridge, David
E-26 1U
07-30-72

Brent, William "Josh"
Fire Pre. Bur.
07-29-85

Bridges, Zachary S.
U/A Batt 2 1U
05-16-99

Brining, John
Retired 3-2-01

Bristle, Daniel D.
E-8 1U
05-16-99

Britford, Bobby
E-6 1U
02-03-86

Broadnax, Terrence L.
E-20 1U
04-09-95

Brooks, Anthony M.
E-1 1U
09-11-94

Brooks, Jerry W.
E-32 3U
07-25-88

Brooks, Kimberly A.
E-24 1U
05-17-98

Brown, Douglas R.
E-22 1U
10-31-99

Brown, Eugene E.
E-29 2U
07-29-85

Brown, Jim
Retired 6-9-01

Brown, Scott D.
R-11 2U
02-04-85

Brumfield, Troy A.
L-32 1U
08-20-91

Bruno, Thomas E.
E-18 1U
11-30-87

Brunton, Don
Retired 6-24-00

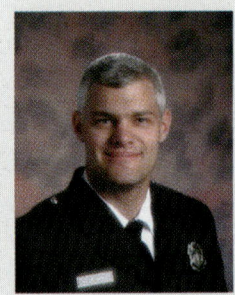

Buchanan, Shawn T.
U/A Batt 2 1U
10-26-98

Burk, Sterling G.
E-20 2U
12-11-89

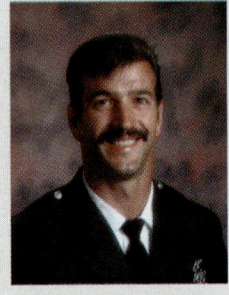

Burnheimer, Michael
E-7 3U
07-26-92

Burt, David A.
E-16 2U
05-19-96

Burton, Robert C.
L-32 3U
07-25-88

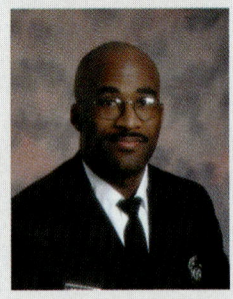

Burwell, William M.
E-8 2U
03-03-91

Butcher, Roger W.
E-7 2U
03-28-88

Butchko, John G.
E-22 1U
06-14-93

Butler, Gerald C.
E-4 3U
10-31-99

Bycofski, Larry F. II
L-22 2U
03-28-88

Byer, John A.
L-32 3U
08-20-91

Byer, Kenneth L.
E-22 3U
05-17-98

Cagle, Stephen A.
E-5 3U
09-11-94

158

Cahill, Richard J. E-31 3U 10-29-79	Cain, Marc P. R-17 3U 12-11-89	Caine, Thomas I. IV L-15 2U 07-26-92	Caldwell, Kenneth Jr. L-10 1U 07-26-92	 Cameron, William K. L-12 2U 06-14-93	 Caplinger, Edward A. FAO 3U 08-20-91
 Capretta, Chad C. U/A Batt 1 2U 05-16-99	 Capretta, John M. E-1 2U 05-04-97	 Capuana, Barbara L. E-30 2U 03-28-88	 Carl, Todd A. L-1 1U 07-13-87	 Carlisle, Robert P. E-23 3U 10-26-98	 Carson, Daniel A. L-8 3U 07-25-88
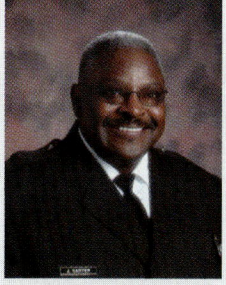 Carter, John H. Fire Pre. Bur. 10-29-79	 Carter, Larry C. E-5 2U 04-12-82	 Carter, Rodney J. E-5 3U 02-04-85	 Carter, William M. E-11 1U 03-16-81	 Cartt, Todd A. E-2 2U 09-10-95	 Carver, Dannie A. U/A Batt 4 1U 10-26-98
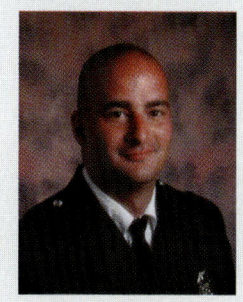 Casa, Tyrone J. E-7 2U 09-10-95	 Castle, Dale B. E-9 1U 12-15-96	 Cates, Elbert L. Sta. 24 40hr. 08-07-89	 Cavener, Kevin J. E-24 1U 11-30-87	 Cecil, Glenn A. L-22 1U 10-31-99	 Cerny, Thomas M. E-18 3U 01-28-96
 Chambers, Harold J. E-21 1U 10-31-99	 Chandler, Paul J. U/A Batt 2 1U 05-16-99	 Charles, Jeffrey A. U/A Batt 7 3U 10-26-98	 Chatman, Nathaniel L-28 1U 04-03-78	 Cheatham, John R. E-23 3U 10-01-73	 Cherascot, Albert A. L-27 1 05-17-98

FIREFIGHTERS — CAHILL • CHERASCOT

159

CHINN • COOPER

FIREFIGHTERS

Chinn, Daniel S.
E-12 3U
11-30-87

Church, Gary A.
L-23 2U
04-07-80

Clark, Jimmy D.
Fire Pre. Bur.
02-03-86

Clark, Perry R.
L-22 3U
01-28-96

Cleary, Jon

Cleary, Joseph B.
E-8 1U
07-13-87

Clements, Christopher
E-19 3U
08-20-91

Clevenger, Bruce E.
E-18 2U
07-26-92

Coffey, Dennis K.
L-13 1U
08-07-89

Coffman, Roger P.
E-33 1U
04-03-89

Colbert, Billy C. II
E-5 3U
06-14-93

Collett, Stanley D.
E-8 3U
10-26-98

Collins, John J.
U/A Batt 5 1U
05-16-99

Combs, Sheldon S.*
E-21 2U
12-11-89

Comer, Robert R.
U/A Batt 2 2U
05-16-99

Conaway, Brian C.
E-16 2U
10-26-98

Conkel, Dwayne E.
E-10 3U
12-14-97

Connell, Kevin R.
E-2 3U
09-11-94

Conti, Andrew J.
E-28 3U
07-26-92

Conway, Joseph B.
E-14 3U
06-14-93

Conway, Joseph C.
E-12 3U
11-28-88

Cooper, Johnny E.
L-15 2U
06-14-93

Cooper, Robert L. II
E-18 2U
03-03-91

Cooper, Spencer R.
E-15 3U
08-20-91

160

Cordle, Jeff
E-2 2U
12-14-97

Cornett, Terry J.
Fire Pre. Bur.
02-03-86

Coss, Bryan M.
U/A Batt 1 2U
05-16-99

Couch, Gregory E-
11 3U
10-16-89

Cox, Aaron W.
E-8 2U
12-15-96

Cox, Clint C.
E-1 3U
09-10-95

Cox, Gary C. Jr.
L-10 3U
07-25-88

Cox, John C.
E-26 3U
07-29-85

Cox, John H. Jr.
L-23 3U
05-04-97

Cox, Scott S.
U/A Batt 2 3U
05-16-99

Cox, Stephen E.
E-12 1U
05-04-97

Crego, Kirk A.
E-4 3U
09-10-95

Cronin, Thomas A.
E-26 3U
04-09-95

Crosby, Russell A.
E-29 3U
01-28-96

Croswell, James F.
E-19 3U
05-04-97

Cua, John R.
FAO 2U
01-26-87

Cummings, David S.
E-13 3U
08-20-91

Cummings, Michael
E-7 3U
10-31-71

Cunningham, Carl L.
E-27 3U
05-17-98

D´Amico, Joseph A.
L-13 1U
04-07-80

FIREFIGHTERS

CORDLE • D´AMICO

Dassylva • Dickson

Firefighters

Dassylva, Robert A.
E-21 3U
05-04-97

Daum, Kevin M.
E-30 3U
01-26-87

Daum, Randal L.
E-32 3U
12-11-89

Davis, Herman D.
E-16 2U
03-13-94

Davis, Joseph E.
L-28 2U
05-04-97

Davis, Morris Jr.
L-26 2U
07-29-85

Davis, Paul M.
E-22 3U
07-29-85

Davis, Timothy A.
E-12 3U
04-03-89

Deboard, Everett D.
E-4 2U
02-03-86

Decarlo, Carmen V.
E-11 3U
06-14-93

Defrancisco, Frank M.
Fire Pre. Bur.
11-30-87

Defrancisco, Peter N.
E-29 2U
10-31-71

Deibel, Michael W.
E-26 3U
09-11-94

Del Tosto, Mark J. •
E-11 3U
04-09-95

Delong, Timothy A.
E-14 1U
11-28-88

Delph, John W.
R-11 1U
11-28-88

Deluca, Bernard J.
L-13 2U
04-09-95

Dennis, Richard M.
FAO 2U
03-28-88

Dennis, Timothy E.
L-32 3U
01-28-96

Derugen, Thomas L.
E-1 2U
05-04-97

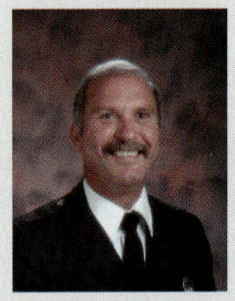

Deskins, Paul T.
L-1 3U
07-29-85

Detrow, James L.
E-7 3U
05-19-96

Devilbiss, Phillip A.
E-13 3U
08-07-89

Devlin, Sean A.
L-2 3U
12-14-97

Dewey, Curt S.
R-16 2U
11-28-88

Dewitt, Daniel P.
E-29 2U
11-30-87

Dewitt, John K.
E-3 2U
07-26-92

Dhume, Jeffrey M.
E-18 3U
12-15-96

Dickson, Paul F.
E-21 2U
09-11-94

Dickson, Robert L.
E-27 1U
03-28-88

162

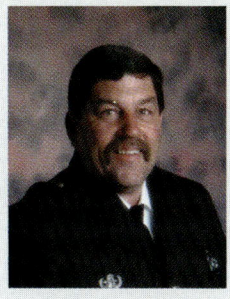

Dill, John R. R-2 1U 10-14-75	Dipasquale, Richard E-8 2U 09-11-94	Dixon, Anthony G. L-15 3U 08-07-89
Dixon, Jill K. E-21 1U 05-16-99	Dixon, Mark E. E-27 1U 03-28-88	Dolder, Tab B. Sta. 30 40hr. 07-25-88
Dolder, Troy D. E-32 2U 04-03-89	Dollison, Mark D. E-28 3U 01-28-96	Donahoe, J. Michael E-22 1U 05-04-97
Dorn, Dorothy A. E-12 1U 12-11-89	Dorsey, Michael I. E-10 3U 12-14-97	Dreisbach, Dennis M. E-30 1U 12-14-97
Ducharme, Daniel A. E-31 2U 07-25-88	Duff, Frank D. Jr. E-10 1U 09-11-94	Duncan, Kevyn B. E-23 2U 12-14-97
Durbin, Tim E-6 2U 09-11-94	Easter, Charles R. FAO 05-15-66 Retired 7-13-01	Eberts, Michael E. E-18 1U 11-28-88
Eblin, James R. Jr. E-14 3U 12-11-89	Eblin, Steven A. E-8 3U 05-17-98	Eckel, David M. L-2 1U 03-03-91
Eckel, Don R. E-33 1U 10-26-98	Eldred, Edward W. II L-8 2U 03-16-81	Elflein, Robert J. E-3 1U 03-30-88
Elford, Laura D. E-15 1U 03-03-91	Ellis, Scott E. E-20 1U 05-17-98	Ellison, Michael W. Fire Pre. Bur. 04-07-80
Elmer, Timothy L. E-13 3U 09-10-95	Emswiler, Dale A. U/A Batt 2 3U 05-16-99	Endicott, John J. U/A Batt 1 3U 05-16-99

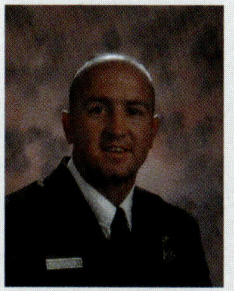

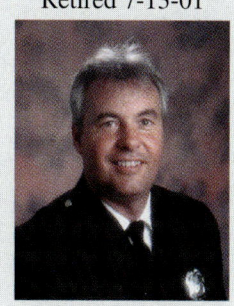

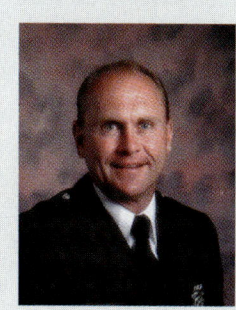

FIREFIGHTERS — DILL • ENDICOTT

163

ENEVOLDSEN • FORD FIREFIGHTERS

Enevoldsen, John K.
L-23 1U
12-15-96

England, Douglas P.
E-27 1U
05-04-97

Estepp, Donald R.
L-27 2U
05-17-98

Evans, Brian E.
Train. Bur.
02-04-85

Evans, Gary L.
Fire Pre. Bur.
04-03-89

Evans, James B.
E-1 2U
07-29-85

Evans, Jeffrey L.
U/A Batt 1 3U
10-26-98

Evans, Mark E.
E-21 1U
02-04-85

Ewing, Edward P.
L-2 1U
07-26-92

Ewing, Joseph E.
L-12 1U
04-03-89

Eyerman, David A.
L-24 3U
11-30-87

Farley, Stephen R.
E-10 1U
03-13-94

Favours, Wilbur P.
L-13 3U
10-17-77

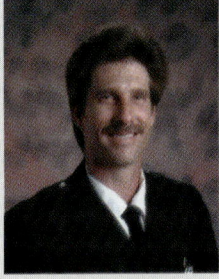

Ferguson, George Jr.
E-7 3U
11-30-87
Retired 7-7-01

Ferguson, Jeffery T.
U/A Batt 7 1U
10-31-99

Ferguson, Norina L.
Recruiting
03-28-83

Ferguson, Patrick R.
E-17 3U
07-26-92

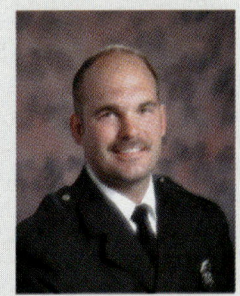

Ferguson, Scott J.
E-12 3U
09-10-95

Ferner, John F.
L-2 2U
02-01-86

Ferris, James C.
U/A Batt 4 2U
12-14-97

Fetch, Michael R.*
L-10 2U
04-03-89

Fields, Christopher T.
E-16 2U
01-28-96

Fields, Donald C.
E-20 2U
01-24-77

Fields, Michael D.
E-12 1U
09-10-95

Figgins, Jon C. Jr.
E-1 1U
05-17-98

Filipski, Daniel P.
E-24 3U
12-26-72

Fitzgerald, Ramona K.
Research/Development
02-3-86

Fletcher, Jeffery L.
E-15 2U
05-19-96

Flickinger, Jeffrey H.
E-3 1U
05-04-97

Ford, Harold K.
E-1 3U
04-09-95

164

Foster, Clifford
R-11 3U
10-29-79

Foster, Mark J.
L-1 3U
04-03-89

Fowler, Brian H.
E-20 3U
12-14-97

Fox, Vicki M.
E-32 2U
08-20-91

Francescon, Anthony
E-16 1U
03-13-94

Franklin, Craig C.
E-15 3U
10-17-77

Fritz, Charles E.
E-26 3U
10-31-99

Fulgham, Bryan S.
E-18 3U
03-16-81

Funk, Jeffrey M.
L-26 3U
05-19-96

Funk, Robert W. II
L-24 3U
03-03-91

Gabriel, Chad D.
E-3 2U
04-09-95

Gaillard, Dashiell J.
E-13 1U
10-17-77

Gall, Leo J.
L-8 2U
07-29-85

Galloway, John R.
U/A Batt 4 1U
05-16-99

Gardner, Donald A.
E-29 3U
01-28-96

Garnes, Byron
E-5 1U
10-31-99

Garnett, Gary R.
E-17 1U
04-03-89

Garriott, Ian F.
E-24 3U
12-15-96

Gary, Gregory P.
E-23 2U
07-25-88

Gatley, Daniel
E-19 3U
10-31-99

Gawronski, John J.
E-32 1U
10-15-72

Geitter, Jeffrey J.
E-17 2U
05-19-96

Gerold, David T.
U/A Batt 1 1U
05-16-99

Getreu, Robert L.
L-13 3U
03-28-88

Gilton, Charles L.
Recruiting
04-07-80

Girod, Chad M.
E-28 1U
10-31-99

Gischel, Michael A.
L-22 3U
10-31-99

Given, Paul N.
U/A Batt 7 1U
10-31-99

Goehring, Michael L.
E-29 1U
05-04-97

Gohring, Mark E.
L-10 3U
03-28-88

FIREFIGHTERS — **FOSTER • GOHRING**

GOINGS • GUAY FIREFIGHTERS

Goings, Forest A.
E-7 2U
08-07-89

Good, John J.
E-19 1U
11-30-87

Gool, Gary
E-12 3U
07-25-88

Gordon, Terone M.
E-28 1U
04-09-95

Gossman, Robert F.
E-11 2U
05-17-98

Graney, Keith D.
L-10 2U
01-28-96

Gray, Kevin R.
Supp. Ser. Bur.
10-14-75

Green, Craig W.
E-32 2U
12-15-96

Green, Jeffrey W.
E-6 1U
10-26-98

Green, John D.
E-5 1U
11-28-88

Green, Kelly F.
R-11 3U
07-30-72

Green, Steven M.
E-13 3U
06-14-93

Greenwalt, Harley W.
E-33 3U
12-26-72
Retired 7-7-01

Gregoroff, Dean C.
U/A Batt 6 3U
10-31-99

Greiner, Gary G.
E-19 1U
04-12-82

Griffith, William R.
L-23 3U
12-14-97

Gritter, Todd M.*
E-10 3U
09-11-94

Groff, Bryan W.
E-19 2U
05-04-97

Groom, Matthew R.
U/A Batt 3 2U
05-16-99

Grove, Brian A.
U/A Batt 5 1U
05-16-99

Grubb, William K.
E-33 1U
03-13-94

Guay, Christopher A.
E-31 1U
01-26-87

166

Guay, Patrick R.
E-31 1U
04-03-89

Guerard, William M.
Air Supp. 2U
03-16-81

Guffey, Jason R.
U/A Batt 3 3U
05-16-99

Gutches, Joseph H.
Fire Pre. Bur.
04-07-80

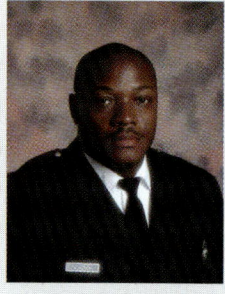

Hadley, Bryant
FAO 3U
02-04-85

Haggit, Gregory G.
Fire Pre. Bur.
01-26-87

Hair, Robert B.
R-17 2U
07-25-88

Haldeman, Andrew L.
R-16 2U
11-28-88

Hale, Robert E.
L-33 3U
10-26-98

Halfhill, Donald R.
L-10 3U
07-29-85

Hall, David H.
E-33 2U
07-26-92

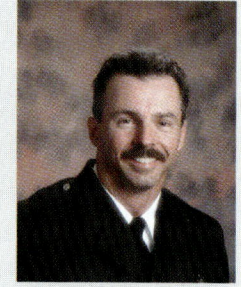

Hall, Richard L.
E-25 3U
06-14-93

Hall, William T.
E-30 1U
03-12-73

Hamilton, Blight T.
L-32 2U
07-29-85

Hamilton, Gary S.*
R-17 1U
07-13-87

Hammel, John J.
R-2 3U
02-03-86

Hammock, Scott A.
E-2 2U
07-29-85

Hammond, Dennis J.
U/A Batt 3 2U
10-31-99

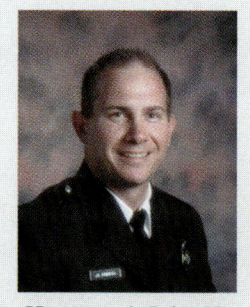

Hammond, John K.
U/A Batt 5 2U
05-16-99

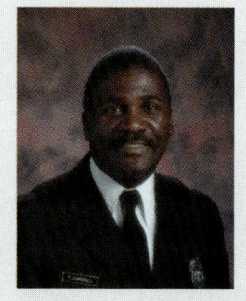

Hammonds, Ronald
L-10 1U
03-28-83

Hampton, Michael
L-28 3U
10-17-77

Hanf, Angela D.
E-25 2U
04-03-89

Hanson, Mark J.
E-16 1U
07-13-87

FIREFIGHTERS

GUAY • HANSON

167

Harding • Helsel

Firefighters

Harding, Richard L.
E-3 3U
04-09-95

Harr, Kevin M.
E-10 2U
03-28-88

Harrington, Dudley F.
E-29 3U
04-03-78

Harris, Frederick H.
Background 40hrs
03-16-81

Harris, Jeff N.
L-15 3U
10-31-99

Harris, Kevin L.
E-24 2U
12-15-96

Harris, Mark T.
E-31 2U
10-15-72

Harris, Patrick E.
E-17 3U
10-31-99

Harrow, Philip L.
U/A Batt 4 2U
05-16-99

Hartman, Richard E.
E-17 1U
03-16-81

Hartman, Timothy G.
E-20 2U
04-07-80

Hartshorn, Timothy
L-27 1U
05-04-97

Hartsoe, David T.
Supp. Ser. Bur.
12-11-78

Harvey, Charles J.
E-32 1U
04-07-80

Hatem, Michael W.
E-17 1U
08-20-91

Hattey, Robert J.
E-14 1U
12-11-89

Hatton, Marc E.
L-24 3U
08-07-89

Hatzo, Terrence S.
Supp. Ser. Bur.
09-12-71

Hawse, John
Retired 6-10-00

Hawthorn, Marc
E-21 3U
09-11-94

Hayden, Kenneth
Firehouse Visitor

Hays, Michael D.
E-26 2U
10-31-99

Heidel, Thomas F.
E-11 1U
12-14-97

Heidelman, Brian J.
E-27 3U
10-31-99

Heil, Shane D.
E-21 1U
05-04-97

Heim, Roger L.
E-14 1U
11-28-88

Helcher, Robert D.
E-12 1U
04-18-71

Helenberger, Frank A.
R-17 3U
09-11-94

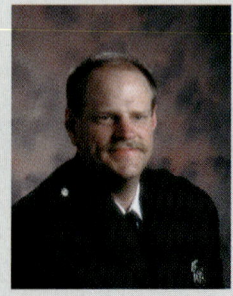

Helphrey, Daniel A. III
E-29 2U
05-04-97

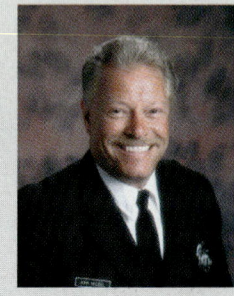

Helsel, John A.
E-26 3U
02-04-85

168

Hendrick, Robert D. E-22 1U 04-12-82	Hennosy, Stephen F. E-10 1U 12-11-89	Herbert, William R. E-18 1U 06-14-93	Herderick, Eric J. E-14 3U 01-24-77	Hernon, Donogh R. E-30 1U 12-14-97	Hernon, Hugh F. E-8 1U 10-26-98
 Herold, Steven M. E-15 2U 09-14-97	 Herrell, Robert J. E-11 3U 10-01-73	 Herring, Jerry R-16 1U 02-03-86	 Herron, Aaron S. E-12 3U 11-28-88	 Hess, Bradley J. E-4 2U 10-26-98	 Heyman, Lance D. E-13 1U 04-03-89
 Hickenbottom, Steven E-30 1U 11-28-88	 Hickman, Tim M. E-16 3U 08-07-89	 Hiles, Christopher B. E-24 1U 09-10-95	 Hill, Kyle M. E-13 2U 09-10-95	 Hill, Mark E. E-18 2U 08-20-91	 Hill, Thomas B. E-27 2U 03-16-81
 Hilleary, Joseph S. L-12 2U 07-26-92	 Hillman, Calvin J. Fire Pre. Bur. 04-12-82	 Hines, Roland P. II L-32 1U 03-13-94	 Hingst, James C. E-19 2U 01-26-87	 Hinkle, Charles E. L-22 3U 12-15-96	 Hinton, Brian N. E-10 2U 12-11-89
 Hobbs, Steven G. E-23 3U 04-09-95	 Hoffman, Dean M. E-25 1U 09-10-95	 Hogg, Eugene M. E-33 3U 11-30-87	 Holbrook, Stephen L. E-1 1U 03-28-88	 Hollis, Donald E-16 2U 01-28-96	 Holmes, Mark E. R-16 1U 11-30-87

FIREFIGHTERS   HENDRICK • HOLMES

HOLT • JAMES   FIREFIGHTERS

Holt, Mark A. Training 25 3U 03-28-83	 Honeycutt, Donald W. E-16 3U 08-07-89	 Hoover, Phillip E. E-29 2U 12-11-89	 Hoston, Melvin C. Fire Pre. Bur. 01-24-77	 Hotchkiss, Douglas E-7 1U 05-17-98	 Houser, Robert M. E-2 1U 04-09-95
 Howard, John J. II L-24 2U 07-29-85	 Howard, Marvin L. Jr. E-5 2U 02-04-85	 Howard, Michael Deceased 6-24-01	 Huff, Laura M. E-4 3U 10-31-99	 Huff, Russell S. E-2 1U 05-04-97	 Huffman, Creig K. E-32 3U 03-03-91
 Hughes, Charles E. E-29 1U 09-11-94	 Hughes, Charles T. R-2 3U 02-03-86	 Humphrey, Bryan A. E-2 2U 04-03-89	 Humphrey, Mark E. L-10 3U 07-25-88	 Humphrey, Matthew J. L-12 3U 07-29-85	 Hunter, Darrell L. E-11 2U 12-11-78
 Huthmaker, Brandon E-21 3U 10-26-98	 Hutton, Robert L. L-12 3U 07-25-88	 Hyer, Scott N. E-18 1U 03-13-94	 Ingram, Anthony R. L-28 1U 04-12-82	 Ison, Steven E-9 2U 12-15-96	 Ivory, John C. Bur. of Admin. 07-29-85
 Jackson, Horace "Bill" E-1 2U 07-26-92	 Jackson, Richard A. U/A Batt 4 2U 10-26-98	 Jackson, Stuart A. E-18 3U 04-07-80	 Jackson, Wallace C. R-4 3U 08-20-91	 Jacobson, Robert A. Jr. E-22 2U 03-28-88	 James, Larry B. E-24 2U 02-02-96

Janiak, Christopher R. E-8 2U 03-13-94	Janoski, James "Matt" E-18 1U 12-15-96	Janoski, John M. E-17 1U 03-13-94	Jarvis, David III E-7 3U 09-11-94	Jefferson, Howard M. L-33 3U 03-16-81	Jeffreys, Fred T. Maint. 34 1U 02-03-86
Jepson, Carl M.* E-18 3U 01-28-96	Jesenovec, Kenneth F. U/A Batt 1 3U 10-26-98	Johnson, Bruce A. E-13 3U 07-25-88	Johnson, Charles M. L-1 1U 02-03-86	Johnson, Jeb A. U/A Batt 3 1U 05-16-99	Johnson, Leroy L. L-24 2U 04-03-78
Johnson, Matthew L. E-19 2U 08-07-89	Johnson, Richard W. E-26 2U 10-31-99	Johnson, Stephen B. L-10 1U 12-11-78	Johnson, Stuart A. L-15 1U 07-29-85	Jones, Louis K. Fire Pre. Bur. 07-29-85	Jones, Richard O. E-5 2U 04-07-80
Jordan, Thomas C. E-30 2U 05-17-98	Julian, John L. E-6 3U 10-26-98	Kahan, James A. E-23 1U 05-04-97	Kaiser, Curtis C. R-11 2U 01-28-96	Kamer, Richard E. E-31 1U 07-26-70	Kaper, Ronald A. Jr. E-15 3U 12-11-89
Karn, David P. R-2 1U 10-01-73	Karn, Robert W. R-16 3U 11-30-87	Karr, Dave L-28 1U 04-12-82	Kasser, James D. E-25 3U 12-14-97	Katona, David E-16 3U 06-14-93	Kauffman, Howard R. E-22 2U 02-03-86

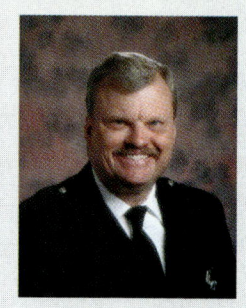

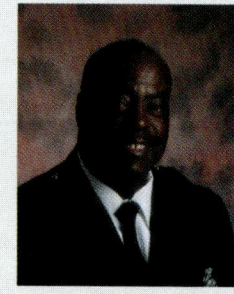

FIREFIGHTERS — JANIAK • KAUFFMAN

KEATING • KESSLER FIREFIGHTERS

Keating, Thomas M.
E-17 1U
04-09-95

Keller, Michael S.
E-6 1U
05-17-98

Kelley, Michael C.
E-24 3U
11-28-88

Kelley, Robert F.
E-28 3U
05-04-97

Kennard, James C.
E-27 2U
01-28-96

Kennedy, Christopher
E-33 1U
10-31-99

Kenther, Michael W.
E-17 3U
11-30-87

Kern, Douglas O.
E-11 2U
01-28-96

Kern, Shannon
E-6 3U
05-19-96

Kerns, Stephen D.
E-1 1U
03-13-94

Kessler, Jeffrey A.
E-23 1U
05-04-97

Keyt, John Q.
E-10 1U
05-04-97

Kiess, Sean L.
L-27 3U
10-31-99

Kincaid, Christopher
E-20 1U
05-04-97

King, Alonzo J. Jr.
L-28 1U
07-29-85

King, Kevin A.
E-13 3U
05-04-97

King, Paul R.
E-24 3U
03-13-94

Kirby, Matthew R.
L-2 1U
11-28-88

Kiser, William M.
E-19 1U
09-10-95

Kiss, Carl L.
L-10 2U
10-26-98

Klein, Christopher S.
E-9 1U
09-10-95

Kleinline, Marc
L-2 3U
07-26-92

Knox, Donald B.
L-26 3U
05-19-96

Kohl, Charles T.
R-2 1U
11-28-88

Koivula, H. Dennis
E-20 1U
12-11-89

Koser, Shawn •
E-10 3U
07-26-92

Kotsko, Joseph C.
E-23 1U
12-15-96

Kramer, Charles L.
E-29 1U
04-07-80

Kranyik, James F. J.
E-13 2U
05-04-97

Kret, Dale R.
U/A Batt 1 3U
05-16-99

Krumm, Matthew L.
E-17 3U
01-26-87

Kruse, Bryan
L-8 2U
06-14-93

FIREFIGHTERS

KEYT • KRUSE

173

KRUSE • LEONARD FIREFIGHTERS

Kruse, Kevin S. E-11 2U 10-31-99	 Kuhn, Richard L. L-2 1U 07-25-88	 Kusan, James D. E-26 3U 10-26-98	 Kynion, Tim L E-25 1U 04-09-95	 Lamb, Stephen W. E-26 1U 07-29-85	 Lammers, Ryan M. E-8 3U 12-14-97
 Landes, Stephen E-5 2U 07-26-92	 Landis, Duane E. Background 40hrs 10-14-75	 Lang, Thomas M. E-23 3U 01-28-96	 Langley, Jeffrey A. U/A Batt 5 3U 05-16-99	 Langwasser, Joseph E-23 2U 01-28-96	 Lascola, Christopher E-16 3U 09-11-94
 Lascola, Thomas A. E-5 3U 05-17-98	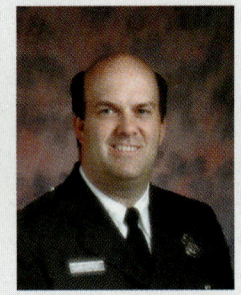 Lathem, Jason A. E-26 1U 12-14-97	 Lathem, Patrick S. E-22 1U 05-17-98	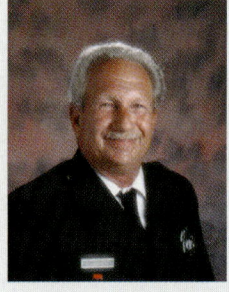 Lathers, Theodore J. E-6 3U 04-19-89	 Latorre, Norman J. E-17 2U 03-13-94	 Lauer, Gregory J. E-20 3U 12-14-97
 Lautzenheiser, Ronald E-4 3U 11-28-88	 Lavalley, Jeffrey L. E-16 1U 07-26-92	 Lawless, Richard L. E-17 1U 02-04-85	 Lawson, Andrew C. E-29 2U 01-28-96	 Laymon, Joshua C. L-27 3U 05-16-99	 Lee, Adrian Y. L-23 2U 09-10-95
 Lee, Rodney D. E-20 2U 08-07-89	 Legg, Dorian E-30 1U 12-14-97	 Kenneth, Legg Retired 6-24-00	 Legg, Richard S. J. E-6 2U 03-13-94	 Leist, Phillip W. U/A Batt 4 3U 10-26-98	 Leonard, David J. E-18 2U 03-13-94

174

Leonard, Thaddeus H. E-28 1U 04-09-95	Lester, Anthony E-17 2U 03-13-94	Letki, Jon Paul J. L-23 3U 10-31-99	Levin, Bret E. E-29 3U 03-03-91	Lewis, Arthur J. Jr. U/A Batt 3 2U 05-16-99	Lewis, Mark A. E-17 2U 03-28-83
Lieb, Joseph P. Jr. E-15 2U 04-07-80	Liebhart, Timothy W. E-24 3U 06-14-93	Lieurance, Paul A. R-4 3U 03-13-94	Liimatta, Kirk P. E-25 1U 06-14-93	Lindberg, Kari M. E-14 1U 01-26-87	Link, Matthew R. E-29 1U 04-03-89
Lint, Barry F. E-20 1U 12-15-96	Livingston, Lawrence L-22 2U 02-03-86	Loeper, Sandra S. E-8 3U 10-26-98	Lofton, Charles A. E-21 2U 04-07-80	Lohr, Michael J. E-10 1U 12-11-89	Long, Daniel J. U/A Batt 4 3U 10-26-98
Long, Tony A. E-23 2U 02-03-86	Longenette, William II E-1 2U 10-26-98	Loper, William W. E-22 1U 10-31-99	Lorentz James W. E-15 3U 05-17-98	Lortz, Richard E. R-11 3U 03-13-94	Loschiavo, Anthony E-32 1U 03-28-83 Retired 8-19-01
Love, Jay D. E-27 2U 05-17-98	Lowe, Chad A. E-21 2U 05-19-96	Lowe, Steven T. L-15 1U 07-26-92	Lowery, Myron M. E-20 3U 03-13-94	Luckett, Curtis L. E-6 2U 05-04-97	Luzader, Richard Retired 1-28-01

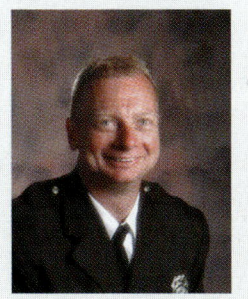

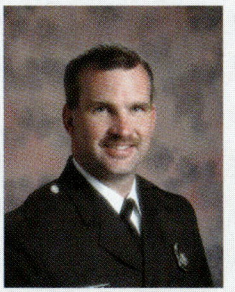

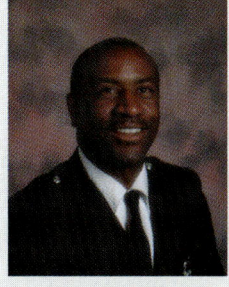

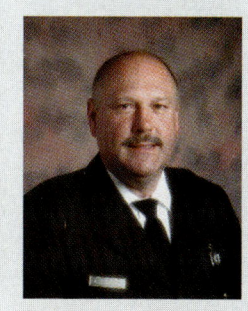

FIREFIGHTERS — **LEONARD • LUZADER**

LYLE • McCOMAS FIREFIGHTERS

Lyle, Teresa A. E-25 2U 03-03-91	Lyon, Jeff D. E-28 1U 10-31-99	Mabry, Ollie E. E-31 1U 04-03-89	Machuga, Charles A. L-12 3U 11-30-87	Mack, Douglas C. L-1 2U 01-26-87	Chief Bill Firehouse Visitor
Mack, Edward A. L-23 1U 07-26-92	Mack, Stuart E. L-1 2U 08-20-91	Malcovsky, Derin A. E-23 2U 03-13-94	Malone, Patrick D. R-17 2U 02-04-85	Malone, Sean P. E-8 3U 10-31-99	Mann, Jay B. L-26 3U 05-19-96
Mantz, Mark A. E-18 2U 03-28-88	Marcum, William R. E-26 1U 12-15-96	Martin, Jeffrey D. L-26 1U 05-19-96	Martin, Paul B. Training Bur. 12-15-96	Massara, Thomas J. R-4 1U 04-09-95	Massey, Joseph M. Jr. E-13 1U 09-11-94
Matheny, Walter C. Supp. Ser. Bur. 01-02-71 Retired 7-6-01	Matthaes, Terry L. Fire Pre. Bur. 07-25-88	Mattingly, Christopher U/A Batt 1 2U 05-16-99	Mattox, Mark E-12 2U 12-14-97	Mauk, Donald E. II E-19 1U 05-17-98	Maurice, Timothy C. L-32 1U 10-31-99
Maxson, Sandra S. E-11 2U 05-16-99	Mayberry, Jason J. E-27 3U 01-28-96	McAninch, Howard E-1 1U 10-01-73	McCabe, Patrick S. L-13 3U 03-28-88	McClain, Jarrod D. U/A Batt 2 2U 05-17-98	McComas, John M. R-17 1U 03-28-88

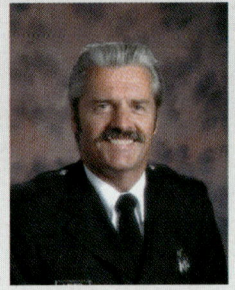

McConnell, Daniel P. E-11 2U 07-13-87	McConnell, Shawn D. E-15 1U 12-14-97	McCunney, Thomas E-24 1U 09-11-94
McFadden, Charles L. E-6 2U 05-16-99	McFadden, John III L-28 2U 04-07-80	McGee, Joseph A. E-12 2U 10-26-98
 McGinnis, Russell A. E-4 2U 12-11-89	 McGue, Thomas M. E-19 3U 05-16-99	 McGuire, Bryan M. E-26 3U 01-28-96
 McKee, David L. E-27 3U 10-31-99	 McKnight, Jason N. E-26 2U 10-26-98	 McLister, David P. R-4 2U 07-13-87
 McNabb, James R. E-8 1U 12-14-97	 McNichols, Max R. E-22 2U 01-02-71	 McNutt, Richard M. L-27 2U 05-04-97
 Meister, Micah P. L-15 3U 10-31-99	 Meno, Mike A. E-13 1U 09-11-94	 Mentel, Daniel P. E-2 2U 12-14-97
 Messer, James E. U/A Batt 4 2U 05-16-99	 Messmer, Lawerence L-22 3U 05-17-98	 Meyer, James T. E-2 3U 08-20-91
 Meyer, John P. E-25 2U 03-13-94	 Meyer, Wayne J. E-8 2U 08-07-89	 Mignogno, Craig P. E-7 3U 12-15-96
 Miles, Michael F. E-24 1U 10-31-99	 Millar, Todd A. R-16 1U 03-13-94	 Miller, Brian J. E-2 3U 05-04-97
 Miller, Douglas A. L-27 3U 12-11-89	 Miller, Edward J. L-2 2U 08-07-89	 Miller, Jeffrey D. E-14 2U 08-07-89

FIREFIGHTERS

McCONNELL • MILLER

MILLER • MONTONEY   FIREFIGHTERS

Miller, Kent C.
E-12 1U
10-31-99

Miller, Matthew D.
Support Services
03-03-91

Miller, Patrick J.
E-7 2U
03-13-94

Miller, Richard J.
E-1 2U
07-26-92

Miller, Schon R.
E-31 1U
03-13-94

Miller, Timothy M.
E-9 3U
12-15-96

Mills, Brian E.
R-16 1U
10-29-79

Minhinnick, Edward
L-28 2U
12-15-96

Misch, William J.
E-13 1U
03-28-88

Mitchel, Robert
E-26 1U
12-14-97

Mixon, Jeffery D.
E-1 2U
03-16-91

Moehrman, Stephen J.
U/A Batt 4 1U
10-31-99

Mollette, Burns O. J
E-22 2U
05-16-99

Molli, Bart A.
U/A Batt 3 3U
10-31-99

Monroe, Daniel L.
L-8 1U
03-16-81

Montecalvo, Thomas
E-9 1U
10-26-98

Montoney, Kenneth
E-29 1U
10-31-99

Moody, Victor E-32 1U 10-14-75	Moore, Dorris E. E-32 3U 05-19-96	Moore, James W. E-15 1U 05-17-98
Moore, Jesse D. E-32 1U 10-26-98	Moore, John R. E-19 3U 05-17-98	Moore, Larry D. L-33 1U 07-29-85
Moore, Michael L-15 1U 07-26-92	Moore, Robert L. E-32 1U 04-07-80	Moore, Robert P. E-5 3U 09-10-95
Moore, Robert V. Jr. L-23 3U 07-26-92	Moore, Scott E. E-33 2U 10-31-99	Morehart, Darren E-15 1U 12-15-96
Morris, Cindy L. E-31 2U 01-26-87	Morris, Patrick L. E-3 3U 04-09-95	Morris, Wayne E-15 2U 05-04-97
Morrison, Chris N. E-21 3U 09-10-95	Morrison, Shannon R. E-9 3U 01-28-96	

FIREFIGHTERS

MOODY • MORRISON

MORSTADT • OHARA

FIREFIGHTERS

Morstadt, Brian A.
E-1 3U
10-26-98

Morton, Thomas L.
Sta. 2 40hr.
10-17-77

Morton, Timothy H.
E-28 2U
12-11-78

Moser, Charles L.
E-16 1U
11-30-87

Moyer, Tad M.
E-10 2U
03-28-88

Munk, Kim B.
E-19 1U
11-30-87

Murphy, Andrew J.
E-8 3U
10-26-98

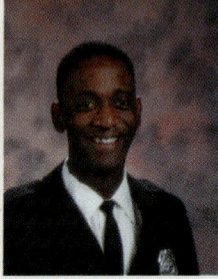

Murphy, Leon D.
Fire Alarm Off. 3U
03-28-83

Murphy, Martin J.
E-8 3U
07-25-88

Musselman, David A.
E-18 1U
08-20-91

Myers, John F.
E-22 1U
05-17-98

Myers, Todd O.
E-31 2U
10-31-99

Nachtrab, John G.
E-20 1U
12-15-96

Napier, Vincent M.
E-22 2U
05-19-96

Neal, John L. Jr.
L-24 3U
12-11-78

Nicodemus, Chad E.
E-7 1U
04-09-95

Niemann, Richard L.
R-4 1U
11-28-88

Nikodem, Robin
12-14-97
Resigned

Norman, Eric M.
R-4 2U
08-20-91

Norris, Martin B.
E-27 1U
05-19-96

Nusken, Matthew K.
E-9 2U
05-19-96

Nye, Daniel A.
E-23 3U
09-10-95

O'Bryan, Shawn M.
L-26 3U
10-26-98

O'Connell, Michael
E-10 2U
9-18-97

Ogg, David A.
E-3 3U
12-11-89

Ohara, Mark S.
L-8 1U
02-04-85

Oiler, Bryan E.
E-10 1U
09-10-95

Olney, Dale E.
E-18 2U
04-03-89

Olney, Lawrence E.
L-27 3U
05-17-98

Ongaro, Edward N. Jr.
E-11 1U
07-25-88

O'Niel, Anthoni M. E-33 2U 05-17-98	O'Neil, Robert E. E-19 2U 05-17-98	O'Reilly, Sean M. • L-10 2U 04-03-89	O'Rourke, Sean T. E-7 1U 11-28-88	Ortiz, Brian J. E-20 1U 12-14-97	Osborne, Rex A. R-17 2U 07-29-85
 Osowski, Brian P. E-28 3U 05-17-98	 Owens, Bradley S. E-18 1U 11-28-88	 Oxley, Gary M. E-15 1U 03-13-94	 Page, Daniel P. E-17 3U 09-11-94	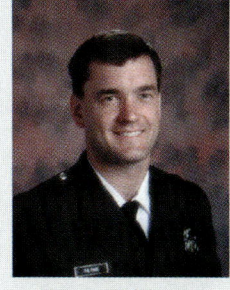 Page, Philip B. U/A Batt 5 1U 10-26-98	 Page, Tommie D. E-28 2U 10-17-77
 Parkinson, Russell R. E-15 1U 12-14-97	 Parrish, Ryan N. E-30 3U 06-14-93	 Parsell, Rodney M. L-26 2U 05-17-98	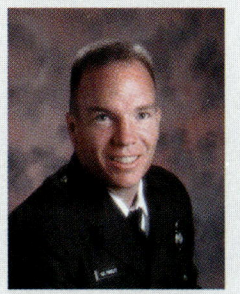 Parsley, Scott R. E-6 3U 05-17-98	 Patterson, James W. E-24 1U 07-26-92	 Paxton, Daniel K. Jr. E-14 1U 01-28-96
 Peck, Loren D. E-5 3U 10-31-99	 Peer, Scott T. E-16 1U 03-03-91	 Peifer, Gary S. L-28 3U 08-20-91	 Pelphrey, Donald E. E-24 2U 12-14-97	 Pence, David C. R-16 3U 06-14-93	 Pendergast, Keith M. E-30 3U 09-10-95
 Penrod, Donald E. E-26 1U 09-10-95	 Pentello, Craig A. L-26 3U 10-26-98	 Perkins, Christopher E-32 1U 02-03-86	 Perkins, Kenneth B. L-27 2U 02-03-86	 Perrin, Leo A. E-17 2U 05-19-96	 Perry, Michael A. E-28 2U 10-26-98

FIREFIGHTERS OILER • PERRY

PETERS • RANKIN   FIREFIGHTERS

Peters, Kenneth R.
E-11 1U
07-25-88

Pettit, Timothy J.
L-12 2U
11-30-87

Pettus, Ned J.
L-33 3U
10-31-99

Pettus, Robert L.
Fire Pre. Bur.
04-07-80

Pfeifer, Lawrence M.
Fire Pre. Bur.
10-01-73

Piccione, John J.
IDC 3U
11-30-87

Pierce, Deidrie
Training Bur.
11-28-88

Pillar, Christopher J.
E-13 2U
05-04-97

Pineda, Robert
E-7 3U
06-14-93

Pinkston, Mark E.
E-15 3U
06-14-93

Pittman, Michael R.
E-5 2U
12-14-97

Pitzer, Jonathan F.
E-30 3U
10-31-99

Pizzurro, John E.
E-7 2U
01-26-87

Planck, Joshua L.
E-27 1U
11-14-99

Plute, David M.
E-27 3U
03-28-88

Poling, Christopher M.
E-8 1U
03-28-88

Porter, Randall J.
E-13 3U
03-13-94

Potter, Darylee C.
E-6 3U
03-03-91

Powell, Michael W.
E-9 3U
09-10-95

Preece, William L.
L-22 1U
03-03-91

Price, Clarence C.
L-10 2U
01-26-87

Priestas, Steven M.
L-24 1U
04-03-78

Primmer, Dennis M.
L-32 2U
11-28-88

Primmer, Jeremy E.
E-12 2U
05-04-97

Pritsel, Charles E.
E-16 1U
03-13-94

Queen, David J.
U/A Batt 6 2U
05-16-99

Queen, Matthew S.
L-2 3U
05-19-96

Rader, Scott D.
L-8 3U
08-07-89

Radwanski, Kevin J.
U/A Batt 5 1U
10-26-98

Rankin, Herbert P.
Fire Pre. Bur.
01-24-77

Ranney, Daniel W. E-17 2U 07-26-92	Ransom, Gary R. Fire Pre. Bur. 11-30-87	Ransom, Timothy L. Fire Alarm Off. 3U 07-29-85	Raver, Ann M. E-25 3U 07-13-87	Raver, Patrick D. L-12 2U 12-11-89	Ream, Michael A. E-19 2U 10-31-99
 Redmond, Tyrone G. E-20 3U 10-29-79	 Reed, Margarita M. E-3 1U 11-30-87	 Reese, Joel A. U/A Batt 1 1U 10-31-99	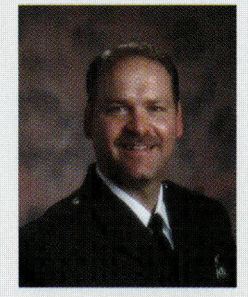 Reeve, John H. E-32 2U 05-04-97	 Reeves, Patrick J. E-25 3U 12-15-96	 Reeves, William J. E-20 3U 06-14-93
 Reinhard, Gregory N. L-27 1U 12-14-97	 Reis, Andrew K. L-15 2U 12-14-97	 Renner, Aaron L. E-6 3U 05-17-98	 Reynard, Roger D. E-6 2U 03-13-94	 Reynolds, David N. L-23 1U 05-04-97	 Rhodes, Gil A. L-26 1U 09-10-95
 Richards, James A. Jr. E-11 1U 12-11-78	 Richards, Paul W. L-13 1U 01-26-87	 Richards, Roger T. E-19 1U 04-09-95	 Riddle, Charles R. E-31 3U 12-14-97	 Rife, David L. L-23 3U 07-13-87	 Rife, Loyd M. Jr. Retired 8-5-00
 Righter, Todd A. E-6 1U 10-26-98	 Riley, Steven L. Jr. E-9 2U 12-14-97	 Rinaldi, Eric L. E-32 3U 10-26-98	 Rine, Carroll Jr. E-24 2U 05-17-98	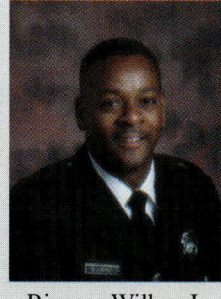 Rippey, Wilbur J. E-20 2U 04-12-82	 Ritterbeck, Edward J. E-18 2U 09-11-94

FIREFIGHTERS — RANNEY • RITTERBECK

Roat • Rossi　　　　　　　　　　　Firefighters

Roat, George W.
E-4 2U
01-28-96

Roback, George T.
E-4 2U
07-26-92

Roberts, John T.
Fire Alarm Off. 3U
05-17-98

Roberts, Theodore J.
Emer. Services
07-25-88

Robertson, Marvin
U/A Batt 4 1U
05-16-99

Robertson, Matthew J.
E-28 1U
10-31-99

Robertson, Stephen H.
E-2 2U
06-14-93

Robinett, Charles
E-8 3U
12-15-96

Robinett, Ernest B.
E-25 1U
05-16-99

Robinson, Charles T.
U/A Batt 6 1U
05-16-99

Robinson, Jeffrey A. II
L-27 1U
12-15-96

Robinson, Jesse N.
L-15 3U
04-12-82

Robinson, Kevin K.
Fire Alarm Off. 3U
07-29-85

Robinson, Monte R.
Fire Pre. Bur.
03-16-81

Roe, David D.
Supp. Ser. Bur.
02-03-86

Rookard, Artie V.
E-5 2U
10-17-77

Rooney, Paul J.
E-5 1U
05-17-98

Rose, Edward D.
E-19 2U
01-24-77

Ross, Jeffrey A.
E-16 3U
12-11-89

Ross, Jeffrey J.
E-25 1U
10-31-99

Rossi, Alexander A.
U/A Batt 1 3U
05-16-99

184

Rousey, Stanley W.
E-12 1U
08-20-91

Roush, Gerald E.
E-28 3U
12-14-97

Roush, Larry E. Jr.
L-12 1U
12-11-78

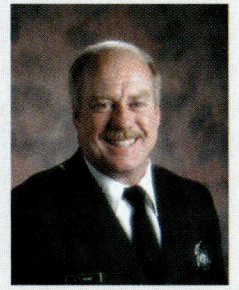

Rowe, Gary T.
E-29 1U
10-14-75

Royer, Wayne A. Jr.
E-4 1U
07-26-92

Rozelle, Reginald E.
L-12 1U
02-04-85

Rucker, Aaron K.
E-27 1U
05-16-99

Ruh, Larry L. Jr.
E-2 1U
09-10-95

Runkle, Victor W.
R-2 3U
10-01-73

Russell, Columbus A.
Fire Alarm Off. 1U
07-29-85

Russell, William T.
IDC 2U
10-14-75

Rutledge, Michael S.
E-12 3U
08-20-91

Rybinski, Thomas J.
E-22 2U
08-07-89

Sachs, Trisha R.
U/A Batt 5 2U
10-26-98

Saksa, Stephen M.
E-14 2U
03-13-94

Salsburey, Donald A.
R-16 2U
03-03-91

Sams, Gregory J.
L-22 1U
05-17-98

Sancin, James R.
E-20 1U
05-17-98

Sanders, Scott R.
E-15 2U
05-19-96

Sanderson, Douglas A.
R-4 3U
11-30-87

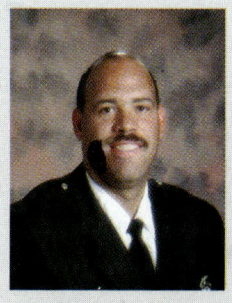

Saniel-Banrey, John A.
E-16 3U
03-03-91

Santavicca, Alexander
E-14 1U
06-14-93

FIREFIGHTERS

ROUSEY • SANTAVICCA

SANTUOMO • SEXTON   FIREFIGHTERS

Santuomo, David P. E-19 3U 01-28-96	 Sauer, Thomas A. E-27 1U 10-31-99	 Sauer, Thomas M. Supp. Ser. Bur. 01-20-69	 Savage, Mark D. E-22 3U 10-31-99	 Sawyers, James Jr. Fire Pre. Bur. 03-16-81	 Scheiderer, Harold J. E-31 1U 10-01-73
 Scheiderer, James M. E-2 1U 08-07-89	 Schilling, Allen A. E-25 2U 10-31-99	 Schmid, Matthew E. E-12 1U 09-11-94	 Schneider, Terry A. E-17 2U 12-11-89	 Schneider, Wade A. R-17 2U 03-28-88	 Scholl, Kevin M. L-12 3U 01-26-87
 Scholl, Thomas J. U/A Batt 7 3U 10-31-99	 Scholz, Kevin S. L-22 2U 11-28-88	 Schrader, Lawrence F. E-13 2U 12-11-89	 Schroeck, Todd A. L-2 2U 08-07-89	 Schumacher, Jack B. E-32 2U 03-17-69	 Schumacher, Jack II B. R-2 2U 01-26-87
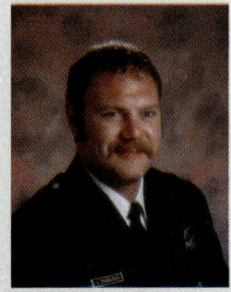 Schumacher, Jay E-7 2U 08-20-91	 Scott, Gerald A. E-12 1U 09-10-95	 Scott, Rickey B. Training Bur. 02-01-86	 Searle, Bryan E. L-10 1U 01-26-87	 Searle, Lynn E. L-1 1U 07-13-87	 Sebert, Jeffrey R. E-22 3U 05-17-98
 Secor, Darren C. U/A Batt 7 2U 05-16-99	 Secrist, Michael N. E-8 1U 05-16-99	 Sedam, Stephen C. E-29 3U 01-28-96	 Seesholtz, Matthew I. E-1 3U 09-10-95	 Selegue, Brian J. L-1 2U 03-03-91	 Sexton, Henry M. E-28 3U 06-14-93

Shafer, Daniel D. E-15 2U 05-19-96	Shaffer, John M. E-25 3U 01-28-96	 Sharp, John W. E-22 3U 08-07-89	Sharpe, Andrew M. E-6 1U 10-31-99	Sharpe, Michael Retired 6-15-00	 Shaw, Jeffrey A. E-15 2U 12-11-89
 Shaw, John D. E-27 2U 05-04-97	 Shawver, Michael F. Supp. Ser. Bur. 10-01-73	 Sheets, Kevin T. E-9 1U 05-19-96	 Shell, Link D. R-4 1U 07-13-87	 Shepherd, David E-24 3U 01-28-96	 Shepherd, Mickey L. E-23 1U 09-10-95
 Shepherd, Paul W. L-8 2U 07-25-88	 Shepherd, Scott A. R-2 2U 01-26-87	 Sheridan, Dennis J. E-21 1U 10-31-99	 Sherman, John R. Fire Alarm Off. 2U 12-20-78	 Sherrod, Donald C. E-33 3U 11-12-73	 Shields, Bob L-2 2U Retired
 Shivers, David L. Fire Alarm Off. 3U 12-15-96	 Sholl, David L. E-23 1U 09-11-94	 Short, Gregory A. E-3 1U 03-28-88	 Siegwardt, Steven A. E-14 2U 07-26-92	 Siemer, Mark S. R-2 3U 07-13-87	 Sierra, Jaime E-31 3U 12-15-96
 Sigillo, Michael A. L-12 1U 01-26-87	 Simmons, St. Julian E-5 3U 03-28-83	 Simpson, Joseph A. E-33 1U 10-31-99	 Sims, Jeffrey A. L-8 3U 07-25-88	 Sims, Keith A. L-10 3U 11-28-88	 Sims, Larry C. Fire Pre. Bur. 12-11-78

FIREFIGHTERS

SHAFER • SIMS

SKINNER • SPENCER FIREFIGHTERS

Skinner, John C. E-33 2U 06-14-93	 Skowvron, Barry A. E-5 1U 04-09-95	 Slatzer, Erin E. E-1 3U 06-14-93	 Slaughter, Carl A. E-28 1U 07-29-85	 Slupski, John Paul L-33 2U 02-03-86	 Smith, Brent J. L-1 3U 04-12-82
 Smith, Clarence D. E-2 3U 04-03-78	 Smith, David E. E-20 2U 05-19-96	 Smith, Jed M. L-22 1U 10-31-99	 Smith, Jeffrey L. E-1 1U 05-17-98	 Smith, Jerome L-15 1U 07-29-85	 Smith, Larry R. E-12 3U 03-28-88
 Smith, Lauren D. F. E-26 2U 05-16-99	 Smith, Lauren Pro. Standards Unit 11-28-88	 Smith, M. Lewis E-22 2U 12-11-89	 Smith, Michael A. U/A Batt 1 2U 05-16-99	 Smith, Philip G. E-23 3U 12-14-97	 Smith, Price M. L-15 2U 02-03-86
 Smith, Robert L. II L-8 3U 11-30-87	 Smith, Steven L. Background 40hrs 03-16-81	 Smith, Timothy E. E-30 2U 07-13-87	 Smith, Tony M. Fire Pre. Bur. 11-13-79	 Smith, Tracy L. E-6 1U 10-26-98	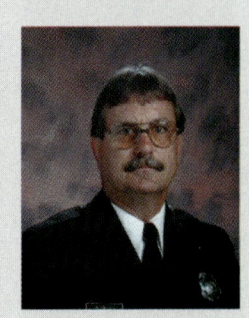 Snyder, Michael Retired 6-9-01
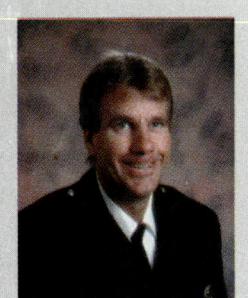 Snyder, Philip L. E-4 1U 04-03-89	 Sollars, Scott J. E-30 1U 10-31-99	 Sowell, Michael W. E-15 3U 10-29-79	 Spafford, Norman E. E-31 2U 04-03-78	 Spellman, David W. E-12 1U 05-19-96	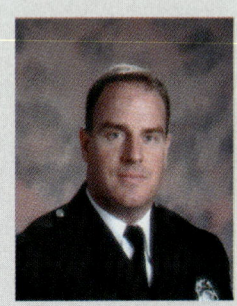 Spencer, Shawn F. E-16 3U 08-20-91

Spradlin, Westly E. R-4 2U 08-20-91	Stanley, Jeffery R. E-2 3U 04-03-89	Stanley, Thomas R. E-23 2U 05-04-97	Starkey, Richard W. E-9 3U 07-13-87	Stermer, Thomas M. U/A Batt 6 3U 05-16-99	Stevens, David K. E-4 1U 07-25-88
Stevens, Sean C. E-10 2U 10-26-98	Stevenson, Tyrone F. Fire Pre. Bur. 04-12-82	Stewart, Danny L. E-18 3U 12-15-96	Stewart, David S. E-25 2U 07-25-88	Stewart, Roderrick E-4 1U 05-17-98	Stiles, David H. L-32 3U 10-31-71
Stimpert, Larry L. E-9 2U 05-19-96	Stone, David C. E-8 2U 11-28-88	Stone, George A. III L-33 3U 08-20-91	Stoner, Keith D. R-11 2U 03-13-94	Storts, Kelly G. E-14 1U 03-28-88	Stout, James M. E-6 3U 12-15-96
Sturgill, Kavin T. L-32 2U 10-31-99	Sullivan, Bryan J. U/A Batt 1 3U 05-16-99	Sullivan, William L. Sta. 28 40hr. 10-29-79	Sundberg, Alexander R-17 1U 03-03-91	Sutton, Jeffrey B. E-2 3U 01-28-96	Swartz, Kristopher T. E-22 2U 05-19-96
Swartz, Ralph E-8 1U 12-14-97	Syx, Robert E. E-15 2U 05-04-97	Szymkowiak, John P. E-20 3U 01-28-96	Talik, Michael L. E-31 1U 10-31-71	Taylor, Douglas R. L-24 2U 05-19-96	Taylor, John R. II E-6 3U 07-25-88

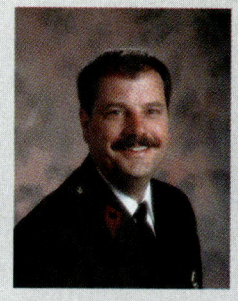

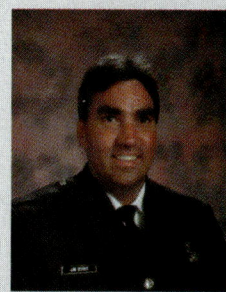

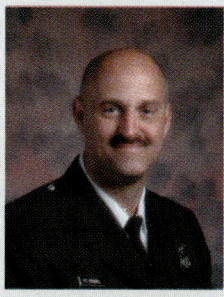

FIREFIGHTERS — SPRADLIN • TAYLOR

TAYLOR • THORNTON　　　　　　　FIREFIGHTERS

Taylor, Robert B.
Sta. 5 40hr.
10-17-77

Temple, Johnny L.
E-29 2U
09-11-94

Thigpen, Steve A.
Facilities Coor. 2U
10-14-75

Thomas, Andrew P.
E-33 3U
03-28-88

Thomas, Keith M.
E-25 2U
03-13-94

Thomas, Philip M.
Training Bur.
12-11-78

Thompson, Daniel P.
E-22 3U
10-31-99

Thompson, Jeffrey E.
E-26 1U
04-09-95

Thompson, Michael
E-30 2U
10-31-99

Thompson, Richard Jr.
E-17 1U
12-11-89

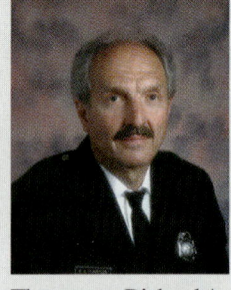

Thompson, Richard A.
Facilities Coor. 1U
05-03-70

Thompson, Robert D.
E-15 3U
10-31-99

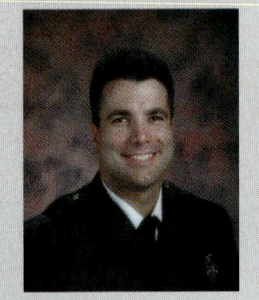

Thompson, Robert J.
E-30 1U
03-13-94

Thompson, Todd R.
E-10 2U
04-09-95

Thompson, Wayne R.
Bur. of Admin.
10-31-71

Thornhill, Michael J.
E-8 1U
10-31-99

Thornton, John A.
E-12 2U
05-04-97

Thornton, Kelly R.
L-22 2U
04-09-95

Throckmorton, John E-24 2U 01-28-96	Thurn, Clement A. Fire Alarm Off. 3U 03-28-88	Tibbs, Douglas D. E-15 1U 12-14-97
Tilson, Ronald E. E-11 1U 01-26-87	Todd, Alan J. E-29 1U 05-04-97	Toops, Harold W. U/A Batt 4 3U 05-16-99
Towns, Samuel E. L-8 2U 02-03-86	Tracy, Daniel J. • E-10 2U 03-13-94	Traikovich, Thomas J. L-24 1U 04-09-95
Trainor, David E.* E-14 2U 08-20-91	Trant, John P. E-14 2U 01-26-87	Trapasso, Salvatore J. R-16 3U 04-03-89
Trees, Shawn M. E-7 1U 07-13-87	Treffert, David L. L-13 2U 12-11-89	Treinish, Steven A. L-2 3U 04-03-89
Trott, Andrew H. L-13 2U 04-09-95	Trott, Craig J. L-24 1U 04-03-89	Trott, Lonnie C. E-33 2U 05-03-70

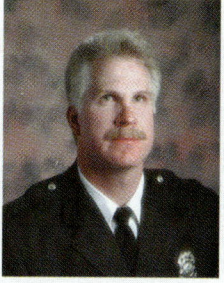

FIREFIGHTERS

THROCKMORTON • TROTT

TUCKER • WALTERS　　　　　　FIREFIGHTERS

Tucker, Glenn E-21 2U 12-14-97	 Tucker, Guy E. R-17 3U 06-14-93	 Tudor, Stuart J. E-17 3U 08-20-91	 Turley, Warren E. U/A Batt 4 1U 10-26-98	 Turner, Kelvin R. L-15 1U 08-07-89	 Turvy, Robert J. Jr. E-30 3U 11-30-87
 Ulery, Anthony V. E-30 3U 10-31-99	 Ulery, David E. E-27 1U 10-31-99	 Vacheresse, John J. L-13 2U 04-03-89	 Vachio, Robert J. L-27 2U 05-04-97	 Vanorder, Scott U/A Batt 5 2U 05-16-99	 Vasbinder, Jack D. E-3 3U 05-17-98
 Vaughn, Tannis E. IDC 1U 10-17-77	 Vedra, Thomas M. E-25 2U 05-04-97	 Vicha, Daniel R.* R-11 3U 03-13-94	 Vincent, Casey C. E-6 2U 10-31-99	 Vincent, D. Jason E-3 2U 05-19-96	 Voit, Michael S. E-19 3U 10-26-98
 Von Ville, Phillip E. E-31 2U 11-30-87	 Wade, Brian A. E-15 1U 05-19-96	 Wadsworth, David L. E-19 1U 05-19-96	 Wadsworth, Jared R. E-7 3U 05-17-98	 Wagner, Rick A. E-32 2U 10-31-99	 Wagner, Thomas R. L-13 1U 11-28-88
 Wake, Thomas D. R-2 1U 04-03-78	 Waldon, Jacob Retired 6-23-01	 Walker, Ronald E. Sr. L-8 1U 04-12-82	 Walsh, William P. L-28 3U 08-07-89	 Walter, David P. L-13 3U 06-14-93	 Walters, Jay E-1 1U 09-11-94

Walters, Larry M. E-26 1U 10-26-98	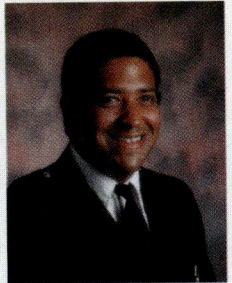 Wandrey, Richard R. L-24 2U 07-25-88	Ward, Donald E. R-4 3U O8-20-91	Ward, John M. E-30 2U 05-17-98	 Wareham, Kent J. L-26 1U 05-19-96	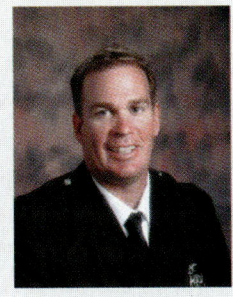 Warner, Rodney R. E-8 2U 12-11-89
 Warnimont, Michael E-12 2U 09-11-94	 Watkins, Herman R. E-21 1U 05-19-96	 Weate, Patrick K. E-17 2U 04-03-89	 Webber, William L. Jr. E-13 1U 07-13-87	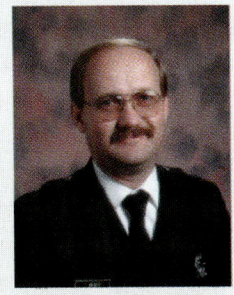 Weber, Tony M. E-32 3U 03-28-88	 Weber, Jason J. E-6 1U 10-31-99
 Webster, Barry E-27 3U 12-14-97	 Weinsziehr, Daniel A. R-4 1U 09-10-95	 Weiskittle, Brian W. E-12 2U 01-28-96	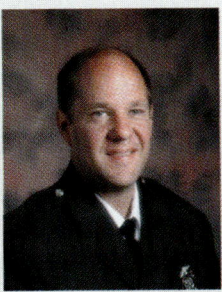 Welch, Gregory M. E-20 2U 01-28-96	 Weller, Timothy T. E-24 2U 05-04-97	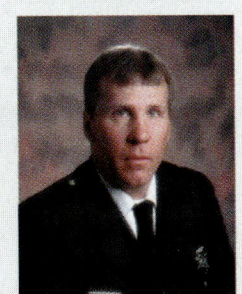 Wells, Gary L. L-1 3U 03-28-88
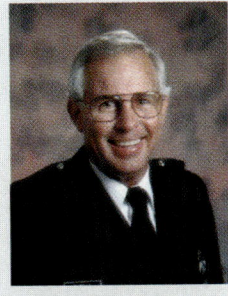 Wells, William K. E-30 2U 10-01-73	 Wendt, Luke F. E-8 2U 04-09-95	 Werchowski, Michael E-11 3U 09-10-95	 West, Joseph D. Sta. 31 40hr. 09-10-95	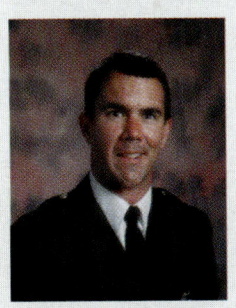 Whalen, James W. L-32 2U 07-25-88	 Whalen, Robert A. U/A Batt 2 2U 05-16-99
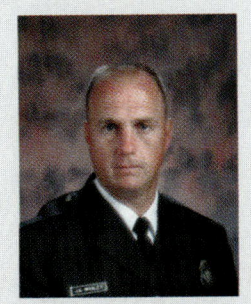 Whaley, James S. L-1 1U 06-14-93	 Wheaton, James E. E-2 1U 09-10-95	 Whetzel, Tod E. E-9 2U 09-11-94	 Whisman, Paul D. E-5 1U 06-14-93	 White, Anthony L. E-20 3U 05-04-97	 White, Craig Fire Alarm Off. 3U 03-28-83

FIREFIGHTERS

WALTERS • WHITE

193

WHITE • WRIGHT FIREFIGHTERS

White, Darrin D. E-28 1U 10-31-99	 White, Kenneth R. E-21 1U 05-19-96	 White, Richard T. E-31 3U 05-04-97	 Whiteside, Danny J. E-17 3U 08-20-91	 Wigle, Ronald P. E-4 1U 06-14-93	 Wildman, Terrance A. E-24 2U 09-10-95
 Wiley, Mark E. E-27 3U 10-31-99	 Williams, Kevin D. L-26 2U 02-04-85	 Williams, Mark A. L-28 2U 10-26-98	 Williams, Terry M. L-1 1U 03-28-88	 Williams, William J. R-17 1U 03-28-83	 Willis, Charles J. E-4 1U 09-10-95
 Windle, Keith J. L-24 1U 07-26-92	 Winegardner, Jeremy E-21 1U 12-14-97	 Wise, Jefferson S. E-10 1U 09-11-94	 Wise, Robert N. E-16 1U 03-28-88	 Wittman, David M. R-2 2U 04-12-82	 Wolf, Bruce B. E-33 1U 10-15-72
 Wolf, Thomas A. E-10 2U 08-20-91	 Wolfe, Kevin D. E-2 1U 09-10-95	 Wolfe, Lawrence E. L-10 2U 07-25-88	 Woltz, Michael D. E-21 2U 10-31-99	 Wonn, Bryan L. E-21 2U 05-17-98	 Wood, Scott E-1 2U 05-04-97
 Woods, Michael L. E-10 2U 05-19-96	 Wooten, Sean M. E-7 2U 09-11-94	 Workman, Matthew L. E-6 1U 10-26-98	 Worley, Kenneth K. E-11 2U 05-16-99	 Wortman, Barry E. E-13 2U 09-10-95	 Wortman, Douglas E. E-16 2U 08-07-89

Wright, Eric S.
L-2 2U
08-20-91

Wyckoff, Timothy A.
E-3 2U
12-14-97

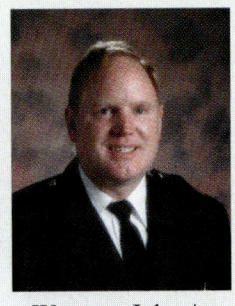

Wynstra, John A.
E-29 2U
07-29-85

Yake, Jeffry
E-31 3U
06-14-93

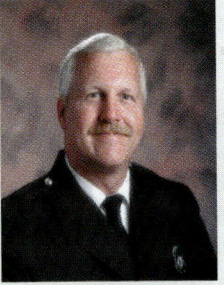

Yeager, Charles E.
E-13 1U
02-04-85

Yerian, Jeffrey M.
L-13 1U
07-26-92

Young, Derrick A.
U/A Batt 2 3U
10-31-99

Young, Michael S.
L-2 1U
08-07-89

Young, Nelvin R.
L-1 3U
08-20-91

Young, Richard R.
E-13 2U
09-11-94

Zwayer, Bradley C.
L-23 2U
12-11-89

Zwayer, James O.
E-26 2U
10-31-99

Zwayer, Kenneth E.
E-4 2U
05-17-98

Zwayer, Mark A.
E-33 1U
04-03-89

* Promoted to Lieutenant in 2001

• Promoted to Lieutenant in 2002

FIREFIGHTERS

WYCKOFF • ZWAYER

CPD
5
SAVINGS HERE
ARE INSURED
WE MAKE F.H.A.
OTHER HOME LOANS
CEN RA OHIO
FEDER SAVINGS

Columbus Division of Fire Civilians

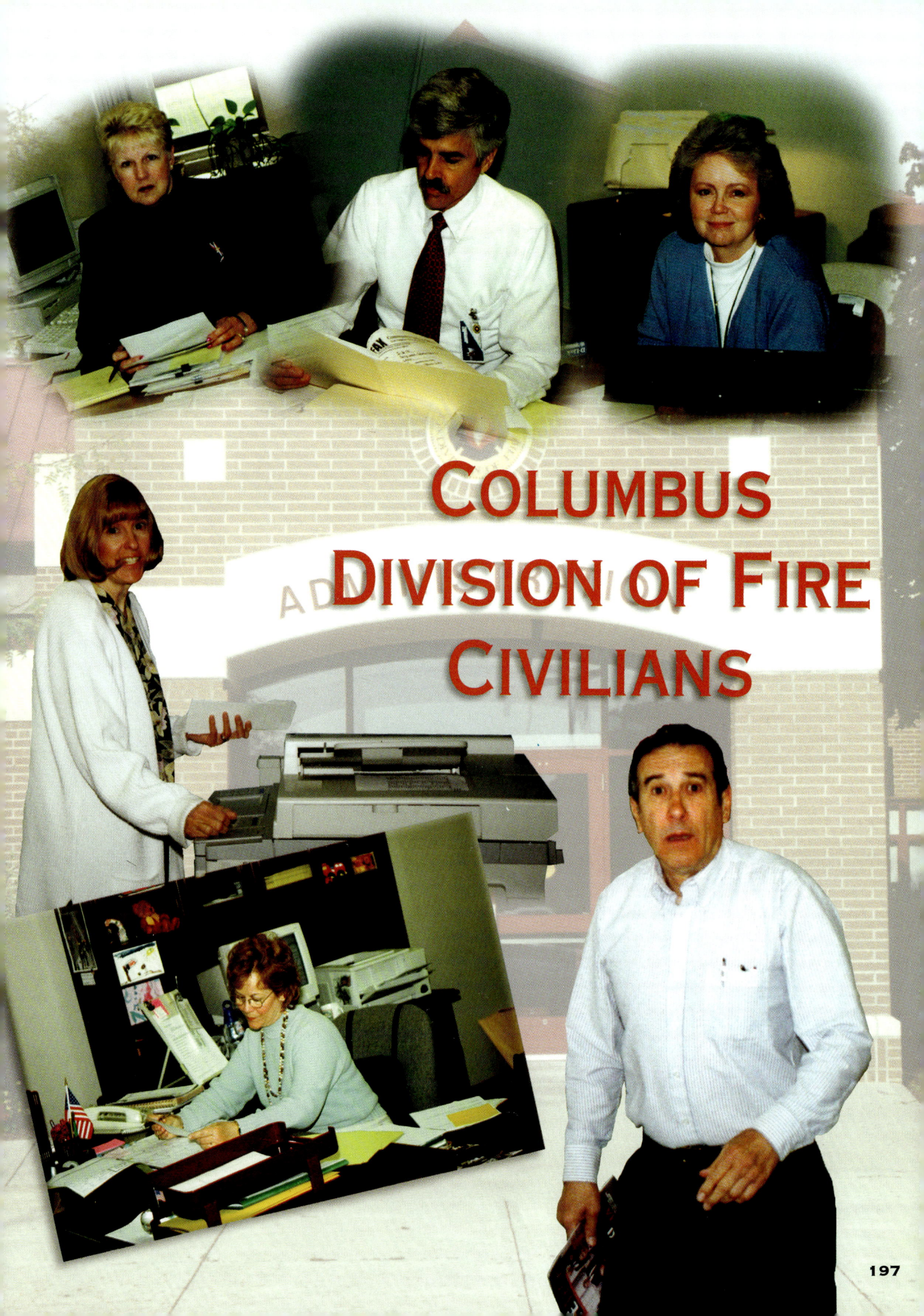

ABBRUZZESE • LEVESQUE CIVILIANS

Abbruzzese, Candy
Purchasing
Coordinator
03-07-99

Atkins, Vickie
Human Resource
Manager
02-21-00

Becker, Barbara A.
Emergency Services
Bureau Secretary
04-04-83

Blue, Christie
Payroll 3U 40hr
Non-Uniform
03-12-00

Botts, Arlene Y.
Accounts
Receivable
11-10-80

Daley, Sabrina
Fabric Repairs
08-31-98

Dunn, Maria M.
Arson Bureau
Secretary
07-26-98

Eaken, Timothy L.
Workers
Compensation
08-01-93

Eblin, Kristine
Fire Investigations
Secretary
09-15-91

Fisher, Lynne A.
Professional
Standards Secretary
08-25-85

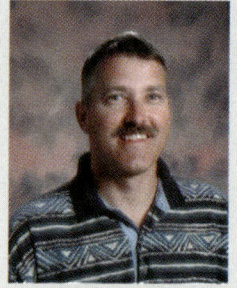

Hamby, Jack
PC Systems
Programmer

Hedges, Janet K.
Fire Prevention
Bureau Secretary
09-01-91

Keseg, David P.
Fire Division
Medical Director
07-12-91

Langer, Teresa A.
Support Services
Bureau Secretary
03-26-95

Leach, Terry
Research/Development
Administration Analyst
01-29-95

Levesque, Sue
Office Manager
11-26-89

Department of Public Safety
COLUMBUS DIVISION OF FIRE
ADMINISTRATION & TRAINING CENTER

1894 SEAGRAVE
HAND DRAWN
HOSE REEL
ON LOAN FROM
CONCORD TOWNSHIP
FIREFIGHTERS ASSOCIATION

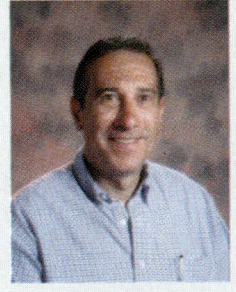

Levy, Jack
Information Systems
Manager

Lopes, Cindy S.
Assistant Personal
Manager
02-08-87

Mackey, Connie
Research/Development
Secretary
12-05-93

Mason, Jill C.
Training Bureau
Secretary
10-01-95

McCoy, Crystal
Fire Data Entry/BIR
02-15-98

McGuire, Kelly A.
Public Information
08-25-99

Peters, Susan A.
Fire Chief Secretary
09-23-85

Rausch, Tondra
Paramedic Coordinator
Retired 2001

Reed, Diana M.
Payroll 2U 40hr
Non-Uniform
10-08-89

Schar, Carol M.
Division
Photographer
03-13-75

Sells, Marilyn K.
Accounts Payable
11-01-98

Sloan, Tina
Union Office
Manager

Taylor, Ronald E.
Supply Supervisor
01-31-96

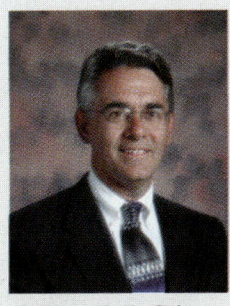

Truesdell, Cris
Business Office
Retired 8-18-01

Waddell, Elizabeth A.
Fire Prevention
Bureau Receptionist
01-23-78

Walker-Greenwald, Debra
Payroll 1U 40hr
Non-Uniform
03-06-95

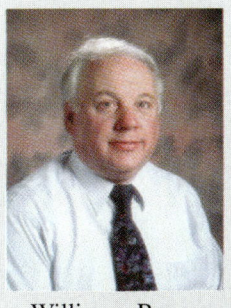

Williams, Roger
Retired

Woods, Sharon L.
Community
Relations Secretary
06-30-91

CIVILIANS

LEVY • WOODS

Personnel Not Pictured

Battalion Chiefs
Balthaser, William E., Batt 6 2U, 04-07-80
Cox, Samuel F., Batt 2 2U, 12-11-78
Lee, Billy G., Batt 4 1U, 10-17-77

Captains
Sprout, Ronald C., L-27 3U, 07-13-87

Lieutenants
Artrip, Rick A., FAO 1U, 11-30-87
Barton, Thomas T., EMS-17 3U, 10-14-75
Castle, Michael A., FAO 2U, 04-03-89
Cox, Gary C. Sr., Air Supp. 3U, 03-12-73
Farson, Thomas B., L-33 2U, 10-17-77
 Retired 10-21-01
Fitzpatrick, William C., E-12 3U, 07-25-88
Graham, Michael C., E-26 1U, 01-26-87
Lee, Gregory, E-33 1U, 01-24-77
Mounts, Kevin J., E-17 1U, 08-07-89
O'Harra, Michael J., E-25 1U, 12-11-89
Ringley, David P., E-1 1U, 07-29-85
Robinson, William E. Jr., E-8 1U, 07-13-87
Sies, Terry R., Supp. Ser. Bur., 01-24-77
Slagle, John R., F-17 3U, 03-28-83
Thomas, Floyd E., Bur. of Admin., 10-14-75
Washington, Gary, FAO 1U, 12-24-73
 Retired 08-19-01

Firefighters
Allen, Darik R., E-15 3U, 08-07-89
Andrews, James R., R-2 2U, 08-07-89
Ayers, Ronald E., FAO 2U, 10-29-79
Bates, Chad A., E-30 2U, 07-23-00*
Bell, Danny J., E-12 2U, 05-04-97
Blackburn, John P., Supp. Ser. Bur., 10-17-77
Bolen, Peter G., L-27 3U, 10-26-98
Brady, Kent E., E-32 2U, 03-03-91
Brintlinger, Timothy U/A Batt 6 2U, 05-14-00*
Brock, Dean A., E-32 3U, 02-04-85
Broughton, Jeffrey A., L-22 2U, 08-07-89
Brown, Rod W., FAO 1U, 03-03-91
Brzezinski, Ryan K., E-14 2U, 03-03-91
Carlisle, Matthew A., E-4 3U, 09-10-95
Carna, Steve M., U/A Batt 4 2U, 05-14-00*
Carr, Michael L., Train. 25 2U, 03-28-88
Cash, John L., E-21 3U, 07-23-00*
Caslin, Lee R. Jr., E-5 3U, 12-11-78
Coey, Ricky A., L-32 3U, 03-28-83
Conley, William E., E-20 3U, 03-28-83
Crum, Dwayne E., U/A Batt 6 2U, 05-14-00*
Cruset, Cory S., E-22 1U, 05-14-00*
Cullison, Thad J., E-18 2U, 12-14-97
Curenton, Kenton, L-28 1U, 07-29-85
Curran, Allen J. Jr., E-11 1U, 03-03-91
Davis, George W., L-10 1U, 07-25-88
Davis, Jason A., U/A Batt 6 2U, 07-23-00*
Dearth, Wayne C. Main. 34 1U, 07-25-88
Decker, Donald E., E-28 3U, 09-10-95
Dommer, Rodney J., U/A Batt 6 2U, 05-14-00*
Dorsett, Timothy L., FAO 1U, 11-28-88
Dye, William R., E-18 3U, 09-11-94
Dye, Leland T., U/A Batt 7 1U, 05-14-00*
Eckenrode, Thomas M., E-26 3U, 07-23-00*
Ellis, Douglas A., FAO 3U, 03-16-81
English, John W., E-33 2U, 12-14-97
Farley, Shawn D., U/A Batt 3 2U, 05-14-00*
Ferguson, Bruce C., E-5 1U, 07-29-85
Gaber, Donald E., U/A Batt 5 3U, 05-14-00*
Garrison, Robin M., E-23 1U, 05-04-97
Gibbons, Edward T., L-2 2U, 04-03-89
Gibson, H. Patrick, E-4 2U, 07-26-92
Gray, James A., U/A Batt 3 1U, 05-14-00*
Greene, Frederick A., E-4 1U, 05-19-96
Hageman, Aaron T., E-25 3U, 07-23-00*
Haile, Anthony L., L-15 2U, 08-07-89
Hall, William D., U/A Batt 1 1U, 05-14-00*
Hammonds, Timothy B., FAO 1U, 02-04-85
Hanf, Holly A., U/A Batt 2 2U, 05-14-00*
Harris, Jeffery A., E-33 2U, 07-29-85
Hart, Melvin D., U/A Batt 6 1U, 07-23-00*
Heath, Douglas J., E-33 3U, 06-14-93
Heller, Roger L., FAO, 10-01-73
Henegar Lonie R., E-4 2U, 05-04-97
Jackson, Christopher L., FAO 3U, 02-03-86
Jackson, Francisca Fire Pre. Bur., 04-12-82
 Retired 10-31-01
James, Donald R., FAO 1U, 04-09-95
Johnson David L., FAO 1U, 07-26-92
Kauffeld Ramdall, U/A Batt 1 1U, 05-14-00*
Kelley, Steven R., E-25 1U, 12-14-97
Kleinline, Thomas, Supp. Ser. Bur., 01-02-71
Knode, Troy N., E-28 1U, 07-23-00*
Kramer George T., L-33 1U, 12-11-89
Kuhlwein, James S., E-14 3U, 11-30-87
Kulpa, Scott H. U/A Batt 3 3U, 07-23-00*
Lambert, Darrell G., E-4 3U, 10-01-73
Lash, Walter A., L-32 1U, 09-10-95
Lash, Lester L., E-5 1U, 05-04-97
Legg, Jon M., E-14 2U, 03-03-91
Lesko, Michael P., U/A Batt 6 1U, 07-23-00*
Lewis, Byron L., FAO 1U, 04-12-82
Lewis, Cornell E., E-9 3U, 05-17-98
Lewright, Dwight L., L-26 2U, 02-03-86
Loeffler, Paul D. Jr., FAO 3U, 12-26-72
Lott, Shane J., E-9 1U, 05-17-98
Madison, Stuart E., U/A Batt 7 3U, 07-23-00*
Martin, Anthony J., E-26 2U, 09-11-94
McCoy, Michael A., Train. Bur., 03-12-73
McCray, Sean T., U/A Batt 3 1U, 05-14-00*
McCurry, Thomas D., E-27 2U, 05-04-97
Meadows, Rick L., Supp. Ser. Bur., 11-28-88
Miller, Deborah L., FAO 2U, 11-28-88
Miller, Nicholas L., FAO 2U, 05-03-70
 Retired 07-21-01
Mitchell, Jeffrey A., E-25 1U, 07-23-00*
Mohler, Melissa A., U/A Batt 7 2U, 05-14-00*
Montgomery, David T., L-12 1U, 07-26-92
Moore, Kenneth F., FAO 1U, 01-26-87
Moore, Caleb S., E-7 1U, 10-29-79
Moore, Virgil A., Fire Pre. Bur., 07-13-87
Moore, John P., Train. 25 1U, 10-14-75
Moree, Cynthia M., FAO 2U, 05-19-96
Morton, Ronald E., E-33 2U, 04-12-82
Myers, Rodney, E-3 1U, 11-28-88
Nelson, William, Jr., U/A Batt 6 1U, 05-14-00*
Ottman, Chad T., E-10 2U, 12-14-97
Page, Carl E., L-33 2U, 03-28-83
Palermo, Michael J., U/A Batt 1 1U, 05-14-00*
Parker, Klaus W., E-29 3U, 04-12-82
Parrish, Matthew D., FAO 3U, 07-26-92
Paxton, Robert J., FAO 1U, 07-13-87
Peer, Stephen W., U/A Batt 7 1U, 05-14-00*
Phillips, Robert L., E-31 2U, 03-28-83
Pontones, Michael, U/A Batt 7 2U, 07-23-00*
Rader, David M., E-4 2U, 12-14-97
Ratcliff, Ricky C., U/A Batt 5 3U, 05-14-00*
Reed, Michael A., U/A Batt 3 3U, 07-23-00*
Reedus, Billy J., Fire Pre. Bur., 10-14-75
Richards, Jeffery A., E-23 1U, 07-29-85
Richardson, Earl R., FAO 1U, 10-29-79
Rickman, George, Jr., Fire Pre. Bur., 03-16-81
Riley, Richard W., L-33 3U, 01-24-77
Robinson, Jeffrey S., L-23 1U, 08-20-91
Rookard, Kenneth J., E-31 2U, 07-23-00*
Ross, Urice Jr., FAO 1U, 12-11-78
Sachs, Denise N., E-5 2U, 08-20-91
Saling, Jared J., E-28 2U, 07-23-00*
Samsonow, Frank D., Main. 34 2U, 03-28-83
Scott, Deric A., U/A Batt 3 2U, 07-23-00*
Seed, Michael S., U/A Batt 6 2U, 05-14-00*
Sendelbach, Charles A., L-13 2U, 09-11-94
Sheridan, Donald W., E-25 3U, 04-03-89
Sheridan, Paul E., E-33 3U, 07-29-85
Shoaf, Joseph M., L-33 2U, 07-25-00*
Snyder, Brian P., U/A Batt 6 2U, 05-14-00*
Spencer, Lloyd E. Jr., Bur. of Admin. 02-04-85
Spiller, Eugene B., FAO 2U, 07-29-85
Stanforth, Jeffrey B., L-22 1U, 07-23-00*
Storts, Michael S., FAO 1U, 10-29-79
Tackett, Kevin, U/A Batt 3 1U, 05-14-00*
Thivener, Fred V. Jr., Fac. Coor. 3U, 05-03-70
Tidwell, Herman, R-11 1U, 07-26-92
Tinnermann, Anthony, U/A Batt 3 2U, 05-14-00*
Turano, Thad A., E-22 3U, 07-23-00*
Wagner, Donald J., E-13 2U, 07-25-88
Ward, James C. III, E-28 2U, 04-12-82
Warren, Henry M., E-27 2U, 01-24-77
Watkins, Mark A., L-15 3U, 10-29-79
Weber, Greg M., U/A Batt 6 2U, 07-23-00*
Werner, Mark A., E-2 3U, 03-03-91
Williams, Michael, FAO 1U, 03-16-81
Williams, Jesse D., E-11 1U, 05-14-00*
Willison, Brian R., FAO 3U, 04-12-82
Wilson, Victor D., Fire Pre. Bur., 03-28-83
Wilson, Brian N., U/A Batt 6 1U, 05-14-00*
Wilson, Christopher S., E-31 3U, 12-14-97
Winbush, Michael, Fire Pre. Bur., 10-17-77
Windon, Michael P., U/A Batt 6 2U, 07-23-00*
Wiseman, Larry D., E-29 3U, 07-14-97
Woessner, Matt B., U/A Batt 3 1U, 07-23-00*
Wolf, Thomas A. E-10 2U, 08-20-91
Woods, Timothy K., L-26 1U, 02-03-86
Woods, Gregory T., U/A Batt 4 1U, 07-23-00*

Civilians
Billiter, Ralph P., Fire Pre. Bur., 02-20-78
Bourne, Geneva C., Bur. of Admin., 10-29-00
Hann, Marian D. Bur. of Admin., 03-08-92
Hetzler, Nappy, Bur. of Admin., 12-04-00
Hockman, Marilyn L., Train. Bur., 09-25-94
Horrmann, William C., BOM, 12-16-85
Hudson, Renee, Fire Pre. Bur., 11-09-98
Knudsen, Peder, Supp. Ser. Bur., 09-25-85
Marburger, Scott, Bur. of Admin., 11-20-00
Miller, Barbara J. Bur. of Admin., 10-22-84
Obrist, April L., Bur. of Admin., 07-06-99
Riedy, Virginia, EMS, 04-30-01
Williams, Robyn D., Train. Bur., 02-15-98
Williams, Juanita, 08-16-71

*Pictured in recruit group photo on page 38.